DEVOTIONAL POLYTHEISM

Devotional Polytheism

An Introduction

Galina Krasskova

SANNGETALL PRESS

Sanngetall Press Valknot design by K.C. Hulsman

Dedication

To House Sankofa, to the Thiasos of the Starry Bull, to Iseum of the Nine Muses and Iseum of the Star*Eyed Warrior, I am grateful for all that I have learned from each and every one of you. You've made me better in my service to my Gods.

To each and every one of you reading this, struggling to learn the ins and outs of devotion, I have been where you are and this book is for you. May it make the work just a little bit easier to follow.

Finally, to my maternal grandmother Linnie Hanna and my adopted mother Fuensanta Plaza: both of you were very different women, but you each taught me about living a life of powerfully engaged devotion. I do this work because each of you, in your own way, taught me well and I am grateful. Mutti, I love you always. Then and now, you sustain. Thank you.

Contents

Preface

This is the book that I wish somebody had given me in 1991 when I was first starting out as a polytheist and in devotional work. For years, I stumbled blindly, trusting the Gods to lead me through — and I was lucky! I had a good living model in my grandmother, good literary models in the literature of the Christian mystics that I knew from my upbringing, and eventually a phenomenal ritual group (Iseum of the Nine Muses) with which to work. Still it was terrifying and wrenching and there were many times I despaired of finding my way through this crazy labyrinth of love and service, devotion, and a deep, deep desire to connect. What does one do with that? It was only years later that I learned of an Estonian proverb: "The work will teach you how to do it," and thought "Aha! So that is what was happening," and it is true, it was, and I do not know if the best guidance in the world could have made it any easier. The path of engaged devotion is rocky and hard at first — we've so much to unlearn before we can learn anything of substance in this work. Before restoration of the self, sometimes there must be unmaking, and so it was with me, and so it will be or has been with many of you reading this. Our world provides precious few guides and most of us come to this work woefully unprepared.

That it is ongoing work often comes as a surprise. The dark places, the valleys, the dark nights of the soul repeat, coming again and again as we move inch by spiritual inch toward our Gods, and likewise toward greater honesty and integrity with ourselves. It is a natural part of the process. In a perfect world we'd have temples and communities and elders and teachers and families steeped — inter-generationally — in devotion, polytheism, piety, and ancestral wisdom. They would circle round and help us as we find our footing on this soul-mountain's climb. They'd support us and guide us and offer counsel when we hit those fallow periods that are such a necessary and normal part of spiritual work. We'd see people who walked this path before us and the desire to do so would be viewed as a good and positive thing within our culture. Instead, what we have is an over-culture that pathologizes devotion and encourages the worst kind of disconnect, entitlement, shallow mediocrity, and rampant materialism. Finding our way in building a devotional life can be daunting. I suppose that makes it all the more precious and cherished when we do manage to scramble onto that road. Certainly we are not alone there; it's been well trod, and here I will have to admit that it's been well trod by polytheists and monotheists alike. There have always been those who looked beyond the cage of dogma to connect to the Gods Themselves. This work, devotional work, is the heart, the beating, pumping, living heart of a tradition, the lifeblood of a faith. I believe it is that for which we were made.

We may not live in a healthy community with inter-generational lines of transmission of tradition and practice, but this book is my way of giving back. It's my way of looking behind me at those standing where I was so many years ago (and where I still sometimes find myself revisiting as I am taken deeper into my work) and extending a hand. This is how I have not only survived but thrived in this work. This is what worked for me. Maybe it will work for you too. Maybe it will provide a piece of a map or a key or a little bit of hope to help bridge the transition into a devotionally centered life. I wish you luck and the blessings of your ancestors as you go.

Before we begin, this book is divided into two parts. Part One explores the ins and outs of developing a devotional practice. While I am Heathen, this is organized in such a way that a polytheist of any stripe may benefit. Part Two is very Heathen focused (though I encourage readers to take the simple rites given there and run with them, adapt them to your own practice, pantheon, and tradition). It provides a week's worth of rituals -- daily rituals to help center one's practice in the here and now – and a series of articles on the holy tides – while these are primarily Heathen focused, many Northern polytheisms share a similar high holiday calendar (since it was based on the agricultural year), and perhaps those of you practicing polytheisms from more southern climes will at least find something useful. Lastly, there is an Appendix which provides a list of questions that I often use with my students when I teach devotional work.

And now, onward and inward…as we begin our journey.

Galina Krasskova
Beacon, NY
August 31, 2014

Introduction

What is devotion? For me, it's the heart of our traditions. This is what makes our faiths live and grow and what infuses them with joy and what opens doors for our Gods to come through. I think it's the most important work that any of us will ever do and I think it's crucial. I talk a lot on my blog about fighting the Filter and I often use martial language but when it comes down to it, each of us takes a stand for our Gods, for our traditions, for wholeness and healing and against what I term the Filter every time we do devotion, every time we pour out an offering, or offer a heartfelt prayer. Moreover, without nurturing one's connection to the Holy Powers…what's the point? I once defined devotion as the art and cultivated practice of loving the Gods and I stand by that. There's a word that I'll use sometimes: *cultus*. This isn't a negative word, not for a Classicist. It refers to acts of devotion, special rituals, and all other ways of paying veneration to a specific Deity. So I'll often write about "paying cultus to" Odin, or Dionysos, or Sekhmet, and this is what I mean: everything that is bound up in consistent veneration. The word however is interesting and I want to indulge myself in an etymological digression for a moment. The word comes from the Latin *'colo, colere, colui'* which means 'to till, tend, or cultivate.' Devotion then is that which one cultivates to develop and maintain right relationship with the Holy powers. The origins of the word itself tell us much about what is necessary to do it well: cultivation, time and energy spent in developing one's practice.

That's the easy part. The hard part is that there's no one right way to do devotion, save respectfully. I can't give you a 1-2-3 set of rules to follow, or a list of guidelines from which you must never, ever deviate. Devotion is a personal thing and when you do it well, and engage with the Gods in whatever way you're able, you'll find it takes on a life of its own. It can be very different for each individual too. This book, therefore, is designed to help one get started, because there are techniques and practices that enrich this whole process and make it much, much easier in the long run. All them will not work for everyone, but part of developing a devotional practice is figuring out what works best for you and then putting it into productive practice. The only things that I have found to be universal are the need for respect and the benefit of consistency.

The core of devotional practice is interiority. There is a whole literature in Christian mysticism that discusses this (most notably Teresa of Avila's work, St. John the Divine, certain Rhine mystics, Meister Eckhart, et al.). Having read a substantial amount of Sufi poetry, I suspect the same holds true in Islam. We have tantalizing hints from various polytheistic traditions, but in many cases whatever written texts there might have been did not come down to us, and many of our ancestral traditions were predominantly oral, which means this wouldn't have been written down in the first place. One would learn from elders, from the community, from peers organically and by osmosis. One of the things that we sorely lack in contemporary polytheisms is that inter-generational means of culture and knowledge transmission. So we have to do things a little more self-consciously: hence books like this. It's a stop-gap because there is so very little in our dominant cultures that encourages a devotional reality. It takes courage to do this work.

This is all the more so because there is an inherent and often terrifying vulnerability in devotion. Part of what it entails, what's really at its core, is opening oneself up to the experience of the Gods. The way we experience our Gods may be different for each of us, but devotional work is rooted in the desire for that ongoing connection and that can at times be terrifying. Our ancestors understood this. They understood -- on a visceral level that we moderns lack – that the sacred always goes hand in hand with terror. That's why religious scholars like Rudolf Otto, in looking at the experience of the divine presence(s), termed it the numinous "*mysterium tremendum et fascinans*" and philosophers talk about "fear and trembling" before the Gods.

I don't believe that we should approach the Holy Powers with fear, though. Respect and joy, love, and a desire to be in right relationship are so much better for the relationships that you are nurturing. Still, there are times where the experience of the divine can be terrifying and that's okay. It doesn't mean that you've done anything wrong. It means that you have encountered a Presence that by its very nature is other-than-human, bigger, older, and incredibly powerful. My one terrifying moment was meeting Odin in the woods. It laid me out emotionally, intellectually, physically -- I fell to my knees and covered my eyes. It tore me open to Him in ways that I'd never expected and submerged me more deeply in a mystery, in Him and His nature, than I ever thought possible. I came away from that experience forever changed and it was because of the years of devotional practice that I already had under my proverbial belt that I was able to come away intact. I had the tools with which to process the experience and I knew that as challenging as my devotional life might be, as terrifying as any single experience might be, there has always been a deep committed love and joy underpinning it. Devotional experiences can shake and shatter the world, move the ground from beneath our feet, open us up in ways we never, ever conceived of and that is the nature of devotion. It is a good and blessed thing in that it leads to more authenticity of self, and a deeper connection to our Gods and ancestors.

Also, it's important to point out that while for many of us, there will be a mystical quality to our devotion (the emphasis on direct engagement), for some, their devotions may involve some ritual, some offerings, and a lot of right action in the world. We are meant to be in the world and to make it a better place in however we are called – in ways large and very small. Devotion does not mean escaping or withdrawing from the world. As Gandhi said once, "there are no small actions." I think that holds true, most especially in our devotional practices. I also often find that devotional work is cyclical: sometimes I'll be very active (singing, praying, working in the world, etc.) and sometimes very introspective (prayer and meditation). It varies and that's perfectly okay too. I sometimes liken it to the way a muscle works: there is tension and release, push and pull, action and repose. This is good. It gives us a time to process things and a time to apply them in our lives. So pay attention as you go, not just through this book, but in the rest of your devotional lives, to the beauty and harmony of those cycles.

Okay, ready?

Then let's get started.

PART ONE

Chapter 1:
Approaching Devotion

What does devotional practice mean to you? When you read that phrase, what do you think it is? What do you hope to gain by it? Consider these things and maybe even write them down and see if, as you work through this book, your conception of the term and all it entails changes or remains the same.

To begin, I want to posit and answer three very basic questions about devotional work. These were actually sent to me by one of my blog readers and they're good questions, and a good way for us to start this journey.

1. What does devotional work (Ancestral or Deity wise) entail?

2. What is the difference between devotional work and ritual?

3. And finally, "is it normal to feel a bit nervous doing a devotional routine with a deity for the first time?"

Let me take these in order. Firstly, regardless of whether or not you are expressing devotion to your ancestors or to a Deity, devotional work is first a matter of setting side time and attention for them/Them. You have to be willing to make engagement with the sacred a priority. Devotional work at its core teaches us to prioritize the Gods and ancestors over our own pettiness. It teaches us to make Them a central focus of our lives around which everything else revolves (and around which eventually, everything else falls into place). This really does enhance every aspect of one's life, but it also demands a good deal of personal work both internally on oneself (because believe me, issues that need to be addressed will arise as one engages with the Powers – we don't get to be passive aggressive with Them and we don't get to avoid our own healing and growth; these things compromise our usefulness), and externally in however one's devotion manifests.

For most, that will include altar work, regular prayer (not set formulaic prayers necessarily, though these can be lovely, but speaking from the heart to one's Gods and kin), meditation (it's okay to talk, talk, talk, but try to listen once in awhile too), study, and perhaps even what Christians might call 'good works.' I certainly know that some of my ancestors like me to engage with the community via volunteer work and such. It's important for them. Also, it's important for us: it keeps us moving from a place of gratitude and keeps us from getting too wrapped up in our own selves and minds.

Devotion can be a very personal thing too. In addition to all of that, each person may find their devotional relationship with the Powers expressing itself in personally unique ways: painting, dancing, gardening – I knew a woman once who kept a gorgeous garden specifically as an offering to her Goddess – keeping a good house, raising one's children in one's faith, studying a particular subject, behaving rightly and honorably in one's relationships. The everyday is not separate after all from one's devotional life; it is an extension of it.

Perhaps your choice of a career is an outgrowth of your devotional life. I know mine is and I have a friend whose polytheistic husband works in law enforcement and this is very clearly part and parcel of his devotion to his warrior Deity. There's a wonderful quote by Rumi that I use quite a lot: "There are hundreds of ways to kneel and kiss the ground." It's true, there are hundreds of ways, of pathways through which the devotional impulse may flow and it's a matter of working with one's ancestors and Gods to find the devotional currents that are right for you.

Regarding the difference between devotional work and ritual, there are numerous types of rituals. Group rituals are a communal expression of one's devotion to the Gods or ancestors; initiatory rituals mark a change in the status of a person before the Gods and ancestors (and community); some rituals are done alone, some in a group. A ritual is a systematized expression of veneration. It may include repetitive words or gestures or actions, it may have elements prescribed by tradition, it may be utterly extempore. What is important to take away from this is that it is one means of expressing devotion.

In many cases there is a communal element to ritual. It is what one does with others. Of course there are private, personal rituals and these have more to them of the intensity of personal devotion, they touch more on the work that one must do externally and internally when in devotional service to the Powers. The communal rituals celebrate those Powers…it's a different type of devotion. At its best, public or communal rituals are where the fruits of one's personal devotions may be celebrated. Needless to say, I find that group rituals do not in any way take the place of personal work and personal devotion. I suppose the occasional group ritual will suffice if one wants to be the polytheistic equivalent of an Easter and Christmas Catholic, but really, only engaging with the Powers in community rituals is doing yourself and Them a disservice.

My only caveat, which I'll repeat often, is that regardless of the actual techniques employed, the 'best' way to honor any of the Powers is respectfully.

Finally, yes, it is completely normal and even to be expected that one will feel nervous or awkward doing devotional work for the first time. Nothing in our culture prepares us to engage with the Powers in this fashion. Plus, most of us are converts to our polytheistic traditions and there's often either the fear of doing it wrong, or a subconscious guilt instilled in us by our birth religions that must be dealt with during the conversion period. Give it time and consistent engagement. You're learning new skills, building a relationship. That's part of it too: this is a new relationship that you're fostering, one between yourself and your ancestors or yourself and your Gods. All new relationships have their moments of jittery nervousness about them. Just be respectful and keep at it and eventually the nervousness will fade as you grow more rooted in your new tradition.

Before we proceed any further, I want to address a matter of fundamental importance. Despite what some people may think, engaged devotional practice is not just for clergy or mystics. It's a way of life that is open to everyone. It's hard, though, demanding. My partner said it best when he pointed out recently that it's not enough to say you're religious; true piety and religion demands action, consistent, continual action. How are you living your faith? What are you doing for your gods?

One of the things that I've noticed over the years is this idea that prayer and devotion are just for 'specialists.' It's nonsense of course, just another excuse to avoid obligations to the Gods, to avoid doing anything, and to deny oneself a deeply connected spiritual practice. Sadly, within polytheism and paganism there are only a select few doing these things, but that is not how it should be. What I'm talking about when I write or teach about developing an engaged devotional practice, making proper offerings, etc., is basic. It's the base line level of competent veneration that anyone can aspire to.

Relegating essential aspects of faith like prayer and proper libations to the realm of clergy is a nice little way of absolving oneself from doing....anything. It's understandable though when you encounter another piece of steaming hot horse shit that is touted (in Heathenry, especially) more often than I'd like: the idea that the Gods are remote, don't care about, and/or don't interact with us. If that's the case after all, why would one care about devotional work? You really can't tell people who hold this view that it's not the case either....they'll hold to that viewpoint, doggedly unwilling (and perhaps unable) to admit that they might be wrong. And they are wrong, fundamentally and at their core, they're incorrect. The Gods are all around us: ready, willing, and able to engage. I have my theories about why someone would even want to cling to such an idea and personally, I think in many cases it comes down to fear ("What if the Gods do care but not about me?"). It's also a means of avoiding even baseline ritual hospitality or competent ritual. Nice to have a religion where nothing at all spiritual is expected isn't it?

Ironically the same type of Heathens who espouse this particular view would be angry and appalled to know that they have so much in common with many Pagans: they want a religion where there are no standards, no rules, no pesky Gods to curtail our human-centrism, a religion where nothing is expected and nothing must be sacrificed. A friend of mine was once told that "you are not a good person if you put the gods before people," that the Gods are "not as important as real human lives." I've heard this before in various ways in response to my work and that of my colleagues. This, my friends is *the* central schism in our com-munities. Here it is. It's not about Jotuns or UPG, it's not about ordeal or anything else. It's this: what has the greatest priority in your life? Gods or people?

For me, it's the Gods. What people don't seem to realize even when we spell it out for them using very small words, is that by engaging in right relationship and right devotion to the Gods, by prioritizing Them, it changes the way one relates to the world, to humanity. All that devotion carries with it an obligation to address the suffering in your world, your community. It carries with it a massive obligation to wake up and start doing what you can, in whatever small way, to make the world a better place.

◆— · · —— · · —— · · —— · · —— · · —— · · —— · · —— · · —— · ·—◆

Suggestions:

I. At this point it's helpful to begin keeping a journal. It is best if you can write it by hand (I don't know why, but I've never personally gotten the same results emotionally and spiritually from typing). I'd suggest trying to write two or three pages daily on whatever you want with regard to your spiritual work.

Begin your journal by writing about any difficulties, fears, or expectations concerning devotional work. Then write about devotional practices in your family growing up and the expectations (spoken and unspoken) of how this would fit into your life within your birth religion.

II. This is also a good time to start working on creating your own prayer book. This is a project that will take as long as it takes to finish. There's no need to rush. You can use a pretty journal, or you might try creating this book from scratch. (Gesso old pieces of cardboard, paint and decorate them, paste your prayers and insights and then stitch the 'pages' together and voila: a home-made prayer book. There are other ways to properly and more formally bind a handmade book too and a simple internet search will turn up dozens of perfectly workable suggestions.) This is something into which you can put whatever nourishes and nurtures you in your devotional life. It's yours alone. This is the chance to make something that will become a working tool for years and years.

Chapter 2:
Basic Exercises

Before we get into the nuts and bolts of devotional practice, there are a few simple exercises that will help provide a solid foundation from which to work. These exercises are crucially important and they will help greatly with the process of discernment later on. They're all the basic exercises for facilitating what I like to call devotional consciousness. They're basic meditation and/or energy work exercises that are essential to learning to engage cleanly. For those who have stronger psychic sensitivities, these practices can be a real lifeline too. I like to give these really early on because I've found them to be both so foundational and so helpful to cleanly starting the veneration process. Those of you who have read my book *Honoring the Ancestors: A Basic Guide*, will have a head start, since I provide the exercises there as well. I would teach these to every single person I meet if I could, they're that important.

My friend Sophie Reicher has written an excellent little book called *Spiritual Protection*, where she gives a lot of these exercises and I highly recommend it. None of these techniques are at all difficult, but they teach the mind to focus, to hit the appropriate meditative state where really good and productive communication can occur. I recommend doing them for a minimum of ten minutes a day.

The first and most important exercises that one can do are grounding and centering. These two simple exercises are the backbone of any spiritual or esoteric practice. They are also, as noted above, extraordinarily useful for dealing with stress and tension. I've also found that they can be an effective tool in managing a bad temper! I learned how to center in a martial arts class, via a breathing exercise called the 'Four-Fold Breath,' which I shall present here. This is not a difficult exercise. All it takes is time. The breath pattern itself will center you. Centering is a multi-faceted process: it gives you breathing room to effectively act rather than react to what's happening around you; it pinpoints your actual, physical center; it helps you establish a personal boundary, to determine where you end and the outside world begins; it aligns the energetic and physical bodies so that both occupy the same space; and it helps one to cope with and effectively process random emotions and energies to which one might be exposed throughout the day or the work.

To do this breathing exercise, simply inhale four counts, hold four counts, exhale four counts, hold four counts. Do this over and over for about ten minutes. You can do this anywhere. You have to breathe after all!

I recommend practicing this several times a day. The good thing about this exercise is that you can do it while going about your daily business and no one need be the wiser. I like to give myself a mnemonic to remind myself to practice. For instance, you might say "every time I see a silver car, I am going to center, ground, and check my personal shields." That would not be too frequent, by the way. The key is consistency and regularity of practice.

In time, as you breathe, you want to feel all the breath, all the random energies in your body gathering about three inches below the naval. You want to feel the energy gathering in a glowing golden ball at this spot. A student of mine once put it this way: "Basically, centering is 'contemplating your navel!'" She was right too. Be sure to breathe through your diaphragm taking deep, even breaths. Don't rush and don't worry if your mind wanders. Just gently bring it back to the breath. One caveat: large busted women and most men center higher, at the solar plexus and even sometimes in the heart chakra area. There is nothing esoteric about this; it's pure body mechanics and physiology. Find your physical center and that's where your esoteric center should also be. One's center is based on where one's center of gravity is. As I noted above, for most women, that is in the hips, the second chakra area. Some larger, or large busted women, and most men center at the solar plexus or in some cases even higher. Centering creates a necessary boundary: it demarcates where you begin and end and where the outside world begins and ends.

Now, once you're centered and once the energy in your body has been collected, it has to go somewhere. Grounding adds stability, it gives one a connection to the earth; it makes one strong, flexible, and resilient. Basically grounding is just sending all the energy/tension/emotions that have been collected in the body, down into the earth. (Science tells us that everything is energy in motion, which means tension, stress, emotions are energy too and energy can be worked with.) Don't worry if you can't see or feel anything. Start with the mental focus and eventually your awareness of the internal flow of energy will increase.

The easiest grounding exercise to begin with is also, like centering, a breathing exercise. Inhale and feel the energy gathered in your center. Now, as you exhale, feel that energy exiting the body through the root chakra (the perianal area) or through the feet, though I find the root chakra is the more stable point. Some practices place the root right at the end of the tail bone – which is interesting after you've spent thirty years working it at the perineum. Try both and see which one works best for you. There are pros and cons to teach method. Anyway, as you breathe, on the second exhale, feel it entering the earth and branching out into a thick, sturdy network of roots. Continue this imagery for as long as you need to, using each ensuing exhalation to take you further and further into the earth until you feel fully grounded. You can use this visualization and breathing technique to rid your body of tension, stress, even physical pain. I've used it to unknot spasming muscles, imagining that I was inhaling and exhaling through the knot itself.

Now, in time you will want to learn different ways of grounding, and you will find that many of the exercises are primarily visualization exercises. Now don't worry if you're not good at visualizing things – that too is a skill that comes in time. I always had difficulty with it. You may find that the image comes via feelings instead of sight and that's okay too. Just like people have different learning styles -- some being visual, some auditory, some more kinesthetic in various combinations – the same holds true for meditation and energy work. Just start where you start.

Some people find it helpful to send energy down through the feet as they walk. That is a useful secondary grounding technique. The idea is that you're connecting yourself to something bigger than you are, and that something (the earth beneath your feet) can support and sustain you. It gives you a focal point upon which you are an axis. The standard idea with grounding is to be a tree. Once you've gathered the energy at your navel, send it down through the root chakra visualizing a tap root and rich network of smaller roots reaching deep into the earth. The root chakra is where one connects to the earth, to primal life energy. Send all the energy down, timing it to each exhalation, into the earth. See it streaming from your root chakra in a solid golden cord of energy. This cord goes down through the floor, through the foundations of the house and into the earth; it reaches very deeply and with each exhalation, see it branching off like roots of a tree, tying you tightly to the earth.

These two exercises are prerequisites to being able to shield effectively. The only requirement to gaining excellence is practice. As my Russian teacher told me when I was in high school: repetition is the mother of learning. That holds especially true here.

Some people balk at the idea of 'shielding.' It sounds harsh and divisive. In reality shielding is just about maintaining good boundaries and you need personal boundaries to be a healthy human being and to maintain healthy relationships. A shield is a filter, one that you control, that helps in filtering out what is not you, all the stimuli that we face on a day to day basis. For people with strong psychic gifts it's a necessity and for people with lighter talents it's also a good and useful tool to have in one's metaphysical toolbox.

If you're poo-pooing the idea of energy work, then think of this as a mental exercise: visualize or imagine or feel a transparent wall, like plexi-glass, between yourself and others. Try this in your job when a toxic co-worker or client is vexing you: tell yourself that nothing they put off can penetrate that plexi-glass wall. See if it makes a difference in how you emerge from those stressful encounters.

Shielding is all about developing strong, flexible boundaries. I find that the people who have trouble maintaining good boundaries in other areas of their lives usually suck at shielding. They're also the ones who could benefit the most from it and who resist it the most fervently. I once actually had a client say to me, "I don't want to learn to shield. I want to be one with the universe." I'm afraid I was tired, aggravated, and a bit more blunt than I probably should have been: "Yeah, sweetheart. The universe is going to crush you like an empty beer can. Sit the f*ck down and shield." But that's me: spreading diplomacy everywhere I go. The crux of shielding is that boundaries matter. They're good things and to work effectively as emotionally and energetically healthy human beings we need them.

Perhaps it's best to think of a shield as a boundary or filter that you can strengthen or lighten or take down completely depending on the situation. One of the reasons it's so helpful is that it allows you to pinpoint what's you, what's an ancestor, what's Deity, what's white noise from the chaos in the minds around you, etc. It's also good, as I noted above, for stress. So how do you do it? Well, just as you send energy down through the ground, you can pull it up again. I would suggest centering, grounding and then pulling energy up on the inhalation and feeling it rise up around you, fully encasing you. This is the most basic shield. Then you can tweak it to your own specifications. I do not recommend the New Age 'white light' shield for the sole reasons that: (a) it's not very effective; and (b) it's very noticeable. Reicher gives quite a few different shielding techniques in her book and I recommend experimenting. You can even ask your ancestors for help.

While shielding is something of an advanced technique (I recommend focusing on centering and grounding for a few weeks first), one thing that everyone should do often and consistently is cleansing. It's very important when doing spiritual work to keep yourself spiritually and energetically clean. This is one of the ways that we can heighten our spiritual receptivity and what spirit-workers call 'signal clarity:' the ability to receive (in whatever way it happens) and correctly recognize and interpret information, communication, and messages from the Gods, ancestors, and spirits.

There are dozens and dozens of ways to cleanse. The most common is probably a cleansing bath. (If you don't have a bathtub, don't worry. The really traditional way of doing a cleansing bath is to pour the mixture over your head. It's much more comfortable though to add stuff to a hot bath!) A few of my favorites include: (a) adding a can of dark beer to your bath; it totally cleanses the energetic body (German folk custom); (b) one cup of apple cider vinegar, one cup of sea salt; or (c) one cup of Florida Water.

You can also make up various combinations of herbs and add a little rum and call it a day. (The rum, my dear readers, is for the bath, not to drink!) I recommend Cat Yronwode's book *Hoodoo Herb and Root Magic* because it gives appendices that list the spiritual usages of many different herbs and it's easy to mix and match. Usually the formula for most spiritual baths calls for three different ingredients and then a cologne like Florida Water, or rum, or something similar like that. Play around and see what works best. I like cinnamon, frankincense, allspice, a bit of orange water and a dash of rum as a good blessing bath. All those herbs are associated with good fortune and wealth and spiritual abundance. For strictly cleansing, I usually just pour some beer in the bath and call it a day. I might also utilize what the ancient Greeks called *khernips*, lustral water. This is made by lighting several bay leaves on fire and dousing that fire in clean water. The water becomes holy.

I would also suggest showering and changing your clothes as soon as you come in from work. We pick up an awful lot of psychic and energetic gunk in our work day. It's best to be clean from it as soon as possible.

Staying energetically clean is crucial. Not doing so can dramatically impact signal clarity and the ability for good discernment. Above all else, devotional work requires discernment.

Suggestions:

I. Start practicing grounding and centering, and record how it is going in your journal.

II. Take a cleansing bath and likewise record the results.

III. Watch "Return to the Land of Souls" (Available for free at www.cultureunplugged.com/play/8436/Return-to-the-Land-of-Souls).

Chapter 3:
Engagement and Obstacles

This chapter is all about how to begin engaging with the Holy (and the obstacles that can get in the way), though I think that to some degree, every single person reading this already does engage in some way, shape, or form. In essence you'll be building upon and refining something you already do. Preparing yourself is a necessary component of clean engagement. In this chapter, I'll lay out what I teach my in-person students, and how I have found it beneficial to go about this type of work. Keep in mind as you go through this book that devotion is a very individual thing: it is the expression of and development of the relationship between you and a specific Deity, Deities, or ancestors. It's not something that can be neatly compartmentalized. It's all about you communicating with and developing a relationship with the Gods in question, and paying proper homage, and They may want certain things that you'll discover as you go.

Also, it's really, crucially important not to compare your own devotional life with others. This is almost akin to spiritual suicide. I can't emphasize this enough. If you compare your spiritual life to others and allow hurt and envy to fill your heart, you are creating a block to authentic spiritual engagement and you're causing yourself unnecessary pain. This is not a competition or a race. Please, please, please do not look at what person X is getting in terms of their devotional engagement and think "this must mean they're better than I am, or that this Deity loves them more." It doesn't work like that.

I mention this because it's one of the most hurtful things that I see in devotional work. Hell, I've even been there myself. I think most of us go through this at some point or another and I can tell you almost without exception, it can damage your relationship to the Gods, sometimes in ways that are very difficult to come back from. Don't compare. I know we all want to grow in our devotional work and we're each starting at different points, and we each have different gifts, learning styles, communication styles, experiences that we bring to our Gods. Give yourself and Them the gift of trusting and allowing this relationship to evolve naturally. If you do the work, it will happen in a way that is right and good and nourishing for *you*, which may be very different from what person X, Y, or Z has experienced.

When I was writing this, I actually had an experience where I found it rearing its ugly head in me. I found myself wistful and hurting and a little jealous because others in a particular setting in which I'm involved were getting very clear, quick responses from a particular Deity and I was being given something totally different and much more nebulous. I stuck it out and talked to another priest about how I was feeling – lancing the boil and washing that poison away – and got past it and realized I was being given a tremendous gift from the Deity in question, of being able to engage with a very, very old aspect of His nature. I was being given something special for me, something that challenged me and engaged me and made me work to get better in devotion, something that kept me from growing complacent, which is all too easy to do. But first, I had to face the potential harm my own feelings of inadequacy were causing and for no reason at all. So I took it as a reminder to both be more mindful in my own practice and to warn how harmful this can be! I've literally seen people destroy themselves spiritually through this type of envy. It's something to watch out for as you work, and grow, and learn.

Spiritual work is *hard*. Devotional work is challenging on every possible level. It's also one of the most rewarding things you'll ever do, but none of that ever made it easy. There's an Estonian saying that I love that sums things up though: "The work will teach you how to do it." Even though it's difficult, the curative is to dive in and fumble and learn and do and you'll find your footing soon enough. Scary, right?

Well, there are a few techniques that can help. I'm always torn at this point whether to talk about altar work or prayer and meditation first and I've defaulted to the latter. I figure learning the protocols of communication is always a good place to start! That's all prayer is after all: communication with the Gods (or ancestors). You're talking to Them, and every good relationship – be it with another person or with a Deity – is based on clear, consistent, honest communication. Prayer – however you conceive of it – really is fundamental to developing an engaged spirituality. It's at the core of devotional work.

Now prayer has a lot of different forms: there are set prayers (like the rosary), freeform prayers, or it can just be conversation. It may be formal or informal, long or short, extempore or carefully prepared. What is important in all of this is that time be given *for* it. The flip side of prayer is meditation, learning to listen – after all, communication is a two-way street.

My adopted mom used to say that the first prayer was "thank you" and if you can think of nothing else to say (it's perfectly normal to feel a bit awkward when beginning this type of practice anew), perhaps consider starting there. Gratitude is never, ever a bad thing. All devotion begins with this type of reaching out toward the Gods. "Thank you" is not a bad place at all to set that process in motion. (I was always taught that the second prayer is "please.")

Prayer is an act of courage. It invites attention from the Gods. It invites engagement while at the same time nourishing the connection that is already there. An awful lot of formulaic prayers are all about asking for things and I always find this a bit distasteful. Yes, there are times where it's okay to ask for things, but I don't think it's good for every single prayer to constantly be a request. Take some time to say "thank you," or "I love you,' or "I would like to get to know you better." That's where the deepening of your practices comes in. So let the first prayer be one of gratitude and let everything else flow from that.

This doesn't mean, by the way, that we never get angry at our gods. Devotional work often involves (as a prerequisite to engagement) a great deal of personal, inner work and quite frankly that can suck. It can be wrenchingly emotional and sometimes devotion involves personal challenges that at the time seem like sacrifices (and later come to seem like the biggest graces in the world). It's normal to have times where you really wish you could punch the Gods, or yell, or cuss, or throw a raging tantrum. You know what? They're big enough to take that. The worst thing you can do is try to deny or not be honest about the emotions. This is part of devotional life: let Them in. There's no need to pretend that you're not hurt or upset or angry when in fact you are. Share that with Them too and work it out together. Stifling this, or refusing to deal with it, is something else that can just strangle the life out of one's spiritual life.

I've noticed an attitude over the years in Paganism and Polytheism that either prayer is a bad thing, a subservient thing, or it is a Christian thing, or it's something that should be left to specialists (priests, shamans, spiritworkers, mystics, etc). All of this is hog-wash. The earliest known prayers date to ancient Sumer – these are only the ones for which we have written records – and are for a number of Sumerian Deities (Nanna, Inanna, et al.). People have always prayed. It is essential to the human spiritual experience. It does not belong to Christianity alone. Nor is it something that only 'specialists' should do. Prayer is the great equalizer of religious life. It's for everyone and it's no more a thing of subservience than having a conversation with an elder might be, or with someone you love.

This doesn't, of course, mean that we can't have a conflicted relationship with prayer. Sometimes the birth religions that we grow up in are so abusive, so heavy-handed, and spiritually controlling that prayer becomes a punishment, a thing of fear, or a thing to be dreaded. This is something that may well have to be worked through. Sometimes the word itself is enough to trigger resistance.

This is one of the reasons for which I have found that formulaic or 'set' prayers are good to have on hand. They are a comfort – there's a sense of being connected to a tradition, and they give a baseline for all those times when you just don't have the where-withal to do anything else. If I can do nothing else, I can say this prayer or do this set of prayer beads. This can sustain. At the same time, I very much believe this is meant to go hand in hand with ongoing, consistent, free-form conversation: extempore prayer. One doesn't negate the use of the other. In fact, I very much suggest utilizing both in your practice. The formulaic prayers help build consistency and the actual conversation – extempore prayers – build relationship. Both are necessary.

I've written before that prayer is the gateway to devotional practice. The corollary to that is meditation. All the exercises I gave in the previous chapter are types of meditation and they have, in part, as their purpose teaching the discipline of stillness and receptivity to our minds. When we talk, we then hopefully listen to what our conversational partner responds. It's much the same with prayer. With prayer comes the need to listen and it's the meditation – the process of listening – that develops, or begins to, the ability of discernment. So while I recommend centering and grounding before doing any type of spiritual work, indeed as a necessary part of one's day, I also recommend sitting and centering after prayer too. Part of devotional work is developing a devotional consciousness: the receptivity in heart and mind and spirit that allows one to open up to the Holy Powers.

One thing about formulaic prayers is that this type of prayer can bring you into community. They're very special. When I say my daily Orisha prayer, I am doing something that is being repeated by tens of thousands of men and women the world over. When a Catholic prays the rosary, it's the same. We're entering into a community united in devotion to a specific set of Holy powers. One of the tragedies of our traditions having been conquered and eventually all but erased by monotheism is that we've also, in large part, lost our set prayers, and the rituals that may have accompanied them. It's one more thing that makes it difficult to connect as a devotional community, but we can make new prayers, and do our best to restore what we have. The Gods and ancestors haven't forgotten these things, and together I think restoration is more than possible. We just have to work at it, but I am more and more coming to look at that hard work as the debt that is to be paid for our ancestors having allowed or contributed to its dissolution in the first place. It is work that is owed.

Suggestions:

I. Think about the prayers that have nourished you over the years. Consider copying them into your personal prayer book, or perhaps writing a new one that you can say daily.

II. In your journal consider the following: What is prayer to you? Does it have a positive or negative attribution? How do you pray? What difficulties do you have? Analyze your feelings both positive and negative about prayer.

III. This is also the time to begin a regular prayer practice. Greet the Gods in the morning, pray before sleeping, talk during the day, etc.

IV. Continue to meditate for at least ten minutes a day (grounding, centering, etc.).

This next section is something I really didn't want to write. It's a painful topic and not one that I have many answers for addressing. Our hearts are such terribly fragile things, so easily broken, so easily scarred. There are some wounds at the confluence of heart and spirit that seem nearly impossible to heal. Still, I'm being pushed quite hard to write this so …here we go.

There are times when elements of human interactions can cause so much hurt that our relationship with our Gods can be damaged. Sometimes those devotional connections, as longed for as they might be, seem so ephemeral. We live in a world so devoid of spiritual awareness. It seems that so many people are starving for contact with the Gods. Then, when we have it, it's easy to invest that contact with all the power and importance that our human relationships may at times lack.

When we do that, it becomes far too easy to reduce the Gods to Their human counterparts or to transfer our unmet human needs, wants, and longings onto our deity interactions. Some of this is inevitable: we're human and our humanity – such as it is in some cases – is the lens through which we engage with the world and each other, and it allows us a deeply personal connection with the Powers, but sometimes there's nothing inevitable about it. Sometimes it's the peregrination of aching, lonely, and battered hearts, and sometimes it leads to terrible disappointment.

My adopted mom's partner used to say that "if you're disappointed, it's your fault for being 'appointed' in the first place." As a linguist, he would often play with words, so at first I was merely amused by the sauciness of this comment. Then I really thought about it.

Many years ago, a very well-meaning gythia took it upon herself – not being possessed, not being an oracle, not even having particularly good signal clarity (if any at all) – to speak for Freya. She meant well, I'm sure, but she and I had and have very different ethics. We have very different approaches to sexuality and relation-ships. Our values are worlds apart. We have very different devotional relationships to our Gods. We have very different orientations as clergy, and very different lives. I suppose in retro-spect, I expected support and encouragement. Instead, the words she uttered did terrible harm. I was younger then, less sure of myself in the work. I still had a human heart. I was in that perilous time both for any Godspouse and any Godatheow: Odin was revealing Himself not only as a Spouse but also as Owner and 'Boss' and the transition was terribly disorienting and painful, hurtful on a heart level. Then I was also coming to suss out what some of the potential sacrifices might be and that too hurt terribly. I wasn't too far away from my humanity yet, and I was feeling very lost.

The words she uttered damaged me, but worse, for a very long time they damaged my relationship with Odin. As vulnerable as I was at that time, her words struck like a lance and in the wash of agony something happened to me: His presence went away.

So painful was this, for so long, that I actually don't remember much of the year that followed. It is nothing to me other than a haze of terrible pain. The only certainty of my world was gone. The only color. The only brightness. I later learned that Odin had used the hurt my friend's words caused as a powerful lesson, -- in my case, the necessity of not seeking external validation, of not being so desperate for confirmation of my inner truths that I held any human's words higher than the connection that is mine to tend and nourish with my Gods. His voice and His alone should have guided my actions.

There was another lesson there too: I needed to learn what it was like to do the work without the reinforcement of that constant sense of His presence that is the gift of Husband to mortal spouse, that constant contact, and yes, constant validation. I needed to learn to trust Him in the relationship we had wrought. For someone inexperienced in either care or trust, the task was overwhelming. But I learned, by Gods I learned. It was the closest I ever came to ending myself, but I learned and one day, His presence flooded back and drove me to my knees with relief. The repair of that relationship took a bit longer.

Why do I mention this now, over twelve years since it happened? Well, I have talked to many people who have experienced a human hurt (intentional or not...usually just the thoughtless fumbling that all too often defines human interaction) and had that hurt spiral so tremendously out of control that it impacted their relationship with their Gods. Person X did or said something, and Person Y, in a spiritually or emotionally vulnerable state, cast those words or deeds onto the fabric of their devotional life. I could tell more stories here, but those stories that I have heard, stories of such tremendous pain that it makes me cry even now as I type this, are not mine to tell. I'll share my own instead.

Certainly I could talk about the necessity of developing and maintaining clean and clear signal clarity. I could talk about the responsibility a clergy person takes upon him or herself: the psychological power of the position, the desperate need and hope and pain with which people will come seeking care. I'm not going to do that though. Those subjects are for another time. Instead I'm going to talk about how to cope when such a situation happens to you. That's why I was told to write this, I think, in the hope that my words might be useful to someone going through what is a thousand times worse than any dark night of the soul – and I belong to a dark God, I've had my share.

Too many people, coming to shamans or spiritworkers, see only the end result. They see us competent and bold in our work. They don't see what it took to get there. They don't see the parts of the journey that were very much like stumbling along in the darkness, feeling one's way with bloody hands, barefoot, walking on knives. Then, when those newly called into service find themselves fumbling, find themselves going through their own personal hells, find themselves thrust into the terror of fallow periods, or disconnected periods, or their own soul's darkness they too often think that they are alone, that they've done something wrong, that they are lost. There's no need for that. We have all walked the monstrous road alone and weeping in the darkness. Most of us just keep our agonies to ourselves out of shame or pain or a thousand other things...lack of support, lack of comprehension, lack of hope.

I want to talk about what to do when those times come, when human hurts slide themselves into wounds in the fabric of our devotion. I have seen this happen in someone and I have seen it slowly corrode and poison their soul. I have seen them fight from that time forward to maintain pliancy of spirit, openness of heart. I have seen their heart scar and struggle not to become brittle. I have seen them in anguish.

I have seen another, long ago, who had her relationship with her God nearly crushed, her confidence in her *right* to love her God almost torn to shreds. Sometimes people do not come back from this. I almost didn't. But I propose, because I am being pushed by my Gods to do so, that how one deals with this, and how or if one heals is a matter of personal choice.

I hate saying that.

When I was in that place there didn't seem to be anything of choice about it. There didn't seem to be anything to do save to die or to endure and my sense of duty was strong enough to pull me to the latter choice…just. But in retrospect, when I really look into the scarred and twisted passages of my heart (not so scarred and not so twisted anymore), I have to admit that the Gods are right. Sometimes whether or not one allows the errata of human beings to root themselves in one's devotional relationships is a choice. I can choose to hold the words of that human gythia deep in the secret fastness of my heart, allowing them to fester and rot everything they touch, or I can choose to let them go, to move beyond them, to hold to my Gods rather than the words and deeds of others. I can choose to cling to my devotion.

Oh, that sounds so simple, when your world is dying around you. In truth, it's anything but. That truth remains, however: we can choose to prioritize devotion. We can choose to let the human crap go, and we can choose over and over again until we actually manage to do it. I will add, by the way, in the spirit of self-disclosure, that I am absolutely atrocious at doing this.

I think the temptation is always there to hold up human things as a reason to draw away from the Gods. Having any type of deep engagement with the Holy Powers means entering into a relation-ship of radical honesty, integrity, and vulnerability that is positively terrifying. It challenges us to be better human beings. It challenges us to move beyond our egos, beyond our bullshit, beyond our excuses, to transform ourselves from the inside out. That's a tall order and quite often involves facing insecurities, and fears and a thousand other things. It's much easier to be hurt or pissed off.

It's much safer, too.

In fact, I think the temptation is always there to allow human ephemera to slide itself between us and the Gods. It's so hard not to listen to the voices of those in our lives, not to prioritize family, friends, the random authority figure in our world, but I say this with deep certainty: in the face of the Gods, all else should be inconsequential. Certainly not enough to wound and damage us, break and twist us away from true. Nothing should be allowed to stand in the way of our devotion. If the Gods are there, that is where I wish to be. But getting to that point, where that wish was all that informed my heart, took a long, long time. I don't always remember every place I had to tread either.

In the end, I don't know what to counsel. I don't know what to say, except something my sister told me: do your devotions. Just do your devotions. Don't waver. Don't falter. Just do.

To that, I would add: seek the Gods with unending fervor; let nothing impede that, nothing shake it from its center. Choose to do this. That's all it is: ongoing choice.

Make the choice every single day to put the human ephemera aside. Humanity makes fools of us all and we hurt ourselves and each other running roughshod over our world even when we least wish to do so. We are remarkably desperate for connection and remarkably unaware. Hurts will happen. This world can be a beautiful but terrible place. It's easy to lose the thread of one's devotional fire. It's easy to close off but we dare not do that. If we indulge the wish to bind ourselves up with our pain we will be contributing to the ossification of our devotional bonds. We will be responsible for pushing our Gods away. We dare not nurture that bitterness, that pain, that anger in our hearts. We dare not for what it does to us. When the imperfection of our humanity knocks us off our devotional center, no matter how badly it hurts – and make no mistake, I say this knowing it can bring horrendous pain in its wake – we need to choose to shake the dust of those hurts from our shoes and move back into the whirling dance of devotion.

How do to that and what to do with the anger and pain that may have accrued, I don't know. I only know that the curative begins with choosing devotion first. There is an element of choice in this struggle and it's a crucial one.

I have noticed an alarming trend in certain devotional communities and certainly amongst up and coming spiritworkers. I suspect it's probably been an issue for awhile, but from my perspective it's now reaching such a critical mass that I and other spiritworkers are slowly being pushed to address it. I've watched this become more and more of an issue over the past few years and I just shake my head in utter incomprehension. What is this issue? It's the overwhelming need I see in so many spiritworkers coming into the work now for external (and ongoing) validation. It's the constant attention seeking. It's the endless quest for a pat on the head.

Spiritual work is hard. It's the hardest thing that a person will ever commit to doing. It's ongoing, too, from the moment we're born; the only choice we have is how well we choose to step up and actively, consciously, willingly engage. Doing that takes courage. It takes sacrifice, and sometimes it takes some very hard, frighteningly hard choices. I have had to do things, say things, stand up and buck the herd for Odin, for my Gods, in order to remain in right service to Them, that terrified me at the time. But you know what? I'm still here. The world didn't end. The work went on and so did I. Even when I've had to pick myself up after making an error, the world didn't cease to be. So I know how agonizing some of what the Gods ask can be and how terrifying.

What I don't know is what it's like to be: (a) bereft of a sense of Their presence; (b) head-blind; and (c) lacking warrior medicine/ orientation. I fully admit, when I slip into the headspace of a priest instead of a cranky spiritworker, that having a constant sense of Them makes it easier to know if I'm on the right track. Likewise being strongly psi-gifted. Having a shit-ton of warrior medicine makes me able to stand my ground, hold a line, and maintain my duty regardless of how I might feel about it. Those things have really served me well. But, they're also why ten years ago, for a solid year, Odin blocked me from any sense whatsoever of His presence. That was the most horrific year of my life. It wasn't until it was over that I was given to know why it was necessary – even the constant validation of presence is validation and we need to be sure and committed to our path, to walk in a way that nourishes our faith rather than dependent on *any* external pat on the head.

Otherwise, it's not devotion, it's sycophancy. And you know what? The Gods don't want sycophants.

Every so often I think, though, about what it was like to do the work (because while He may have blinded me to His presence, the work and personal spiritual challenges didn't stop – in fact, they increased) without that sense of completion deep in my heart. I think about the grief, the constant aching hunger for some type of connection – anything, the barest wisp – the guilt (what did I do wrong?), and the confusion. This was all with me still being able to sense other Deities, and still being able to divine (so long as I didn't ask anything about my own situation). I am not completely blind to the fear and the sense of desolation that is so often a part of finding one's footing in this work. No one starts out with a fully open set of gifts and talents. We earn them. We develop them. Sometimes we suffer for them. That's part of the work too.

Even for the best spiritworkers and devotees out there, there will be fallow periods. There are times when one is just not feeling as deeply connected. There are times when the Gods and spirits seem very far away. There are times when you have no sense of internal 'course correction' when the question arises "am I doing this right?" Christian mystics referred to this as the 'dark night of the soul' and mystical tradition considers it an essential part of any authentic spiritual crafting (a word I like ever so much better than 'seeking,' because this is our life's masterwork, whether one is a spirit worker, a mystic or just a regular Joe trying to get by). Having a period of disconnection, having a fallow time does not mean you did anything wrong. It is a normal part of the spiritual cycle. I've often found that it means you've done quite a bit right and your spirit is in the process of integrating all the changes, epiphanies, and effects contact with (hell, even plain old seeking) the sacred brings.

How can you ever find your way, or center yourself fully in the road of devotion if you're endlessly willing to change your path on the whim of a random person's say so? How can there ever be integrity in what you do if you're constantly worried about how others are going to respond? I come from a tradition that puts great stock in elders and having elders as maintainers of the lineage, guardians of the tradition. This is well and good and, I believe, necessary. Certainly none of us is evolving and working in a vacuum. We're interconnected whether we want to be or not. We can draw great nourishment from one another – one of the reasons I like talking to colleagues and friends, and other spiritworkers and devotees. There are times when it is right and proper, in moments of spiritual crisis, to go to one's elders to get oneself sorted out. That is a far different cry from posting on Tumblr after every meditation: "I got this when I prayed. Is it right? Does Loki like me? Am I doing this right? Huh? Huh? Huh?" Just stop it. For fuck sake, stop. Are you doing this out of love of the Gods and a desire to serve or are you doing this because you want to be part of what you think is some cool club? Just. Stop. Spirituality makes a really bad hobby.

Furthermore, if your Gods and ancestors are satisfied with your work, then my opinion "don't mean a thing." If they're not satisfied, then I can be telling you you're doing everything fine and that also doesn't mean anything. In fact, I'd be wrong and I'd be responsible on a wyrd level for potentially causing spiritual harm. If you can't figure out if your Gods and ancestors are satisfied, then maybe consult a diviner – but do so to find out what you must do, and do so asking also how you can learn to communicate with Them better. You don't have to be highly psi-gifted to do this work. The work will teach you how to do it and the results will, in time, be apparent. You will gain a sense of whether or not you are in right relationship with your Powers. You'll gain a sense of when you need a 'course correction.' You'll also learn when it's time to consult an elder or diviner. Part of this means developing a backbone.

"Never grow a wishbone, daughter, where your backbone ought to be." This quote by Clemetine Paddleford is something that I actually learned at my adopted mother's knee. She used to keep a copy of this saying – written in her extraordinary calligraphy, which I might add, was her everyday handwriting – hanging in her home. She would refer to it often, and it proved inspiring. She lived its message too, every day of her life. Anyone wanting to do this work well should take note. There's a reason that the first precept at the oracle of Delphi was "Know thyself." There's no getting around this requirement. Know yourself and who the Gods and ancestors want you to be. Know who you want to be…not who your friends, parents, neighbors, or boyfriend might want you to be. For Gods' sake, give over the need to have everyone like you. Spiritual work isn't a social event. When those of us doing this work come together as colleagues, it's to share knowledge, exchange ideas, to enjoy the company of others who walk similar roads, who have been taken up by Gods and spirits and in so many ineffable (and some quite obvious) ways been rendered 'other' in the sad and disjointed world in which we live, a world many of us have been tasked with transforming. We're not coming together to be told we're doing it right.

Recently I was reading a book on women in business. It was mildly interesting but what struck me was a comment the author made about those just entering the workforce (Gen-Y? I can never keep them straight). She commented that this generation has been used to getting a lot of attention from adults, and they don't really grasp necessary hierarchies or the need for hard, solitary work, so they can make faux pas in interviewing situations that take them right out of the running. Putting all the interview advice aside as irrelevant here, I was struck by the generational comment because I do think that's a large part of what we're dealing with in the community. I see this predominantly with younger spiritworkers and devotees…those just reaching adulthood, or in their early to mid twenties. I'm not saying us older folk can't have the same type of nonsense going on, but I've mostly seen it with twenty-somethings. I believe that at least part of this is a generational thing. A lot of attention from adults means a lot of constant feedback and external validation. Add that to a generation that went through a school system that tended to give kids a prize just for showing up (forget about excellence), and who have been raised so coddled and medicated as to have the emotional resiliency of soap bubbles and you have a generation ripe for disaster. There's a learning curve, and for y'all, it can be a big one. Good. Challenges met make success all the sweeter. Learning to forego external validation and attention is a good first offering and challenge, one that will put you in good stead throughout the rest of your spiritual life...i.e., your life.

I also think the fact that most of us are converts to polytheism is coming into play. There's a certain psychology of conversion: one converts and then, in a need to distance him or herself from the birth faith, tries to be "more Pagan than other Pagans." While I'm not seeing that so much here (though I do see a pathetic amount of attempted one-upmanship) what can also happen is a really desperate need to make sure one is doing it 'right.' Monotheism teaches one to look for validation in a book or from a priest, or in gospel or orthodoxy...all external sources. So we default to what is known. Then part of me, a very cynical part, thinks that sometimes the person constantly seeking attention and validation really just wants to foist responsibility for his or her own spiritual life off on someone else. After all, if you don't have to make any choices, if you don't have to live with occasionally making the wrong choices and then having to go back and make it right (or live with the consequences) then it's not so bad after all, is it? Problem is, it doesn't work that way and trying to dump your spiritual shit on random spiritworkers really pisses us off. I'll go to the wall for someone working as hard as he or she can to get right with the Gods and ancestors. No matter how hard that person struggles or screws up, I'll go to the wall for him or her. Many spiritworkers I know feel the same. Working hard and still dropping a few balls is a far cry from abrogating all responsibility for one's spiritual life into one big "just tell me I'm doing good."

We must be bold in loving our Gods. The Sufi mystic Rumi once wrote that "love comes with a knife, not some shy question." That is devotion. That is what falling headfirst into the sacred brings and when it does, it changes everything. First though, there must be courage and a willingness to throw oneself headlong into that abyss. Don't worry, the Gods and ancestors will catch you; and if they don't, it's not such a bad way to go after all.

Chapter 4:
Altar and Shrine Work

I always struggle with what to teach first: prayer/ meditation or altar work. I could make an argument either way, but I usually touch on altars and shrines after prayer – after all, it seems rather rude to invite someone into your life without first having introduced yourself! (Really though, for years, I would suggest altar work first. Six of one, half dozen of the other, I suppose; just start where you start.)

I tend to use the terms 'shrine' and 'altar' interchangeably, but this is not actually correct. It was common parlance when I began as a polytheist, and unfortunately, it's a bad habit I've hung onto. Most traditions that I'm familiar with would separate the two ideas, with a shrine being an all-purpose place of devotion either set up in the home for veneration or perhaps in public (but that is open to communal veneration), and an altar being something that is usually found in a temple (or within a larger shrine) and that has a specific purpose. Again, I use them interchangeably because when I was first starting out, my own teachers simply referred to "altar work" but I want you to understand the difference.

We are creatures of the sensorium and for this and many other reasons I think that shrine work (altar work) is very, very important. A shrine is a living thing. It's a place of reverence and devotion, a place for the active expression of cultic devotion and it's also a place of welcome to the Gods (or ancestors or spirits) in question. It's a focal point, and a mnemonic that our lives are centered around reverence for the Gods.

My own experience with altars and shrines is that of first a priest and then a shaman so it is *not* typical. I have a working altar (though it shifts around a lot – I tend to like to work in my common room because it's close to my ancestor shrine and that just feels nice) and over fifty shrines in my home. I really want to emphasize that you do *not* need to have fifty-plus shrines. Usually an ancestor shrine and one to the gods suffices. Some people are even okay with combining them.

Either way, a shrine or altar is a living thing, a reflection of your own spiritual life and connections. It's a powerful point of welcome, a visual metaphor and message to the Gods in question too: you're opening up to interaction. I find it's also a peaceful place to meditate because over time, as you engage in ongoing veneration, the residual presence of the Gods to Whom the altar/shrine is dedicated become quietly palpable. It becomes a sacred space.

Your altar or shrine should be kept alive and vibrant. There's a verse in the *Havamal* that counsels that the road between friends is often traveled implying that this repetitive contact is significant, it's what keeps that friendship strong – and it's the same with the Gods (or ancestors). In essence, a well-maintained shrine becomes a home for the Deities it honors.

Now, you may have non-polytheistic folks claim that in doing altar work you're "praying to an idol, or worshipping an image." This isn't so. In *Northern Tradition for the Solitary Practitioner*, Raven Kaldera and I wrote:

"We are steeped in ethnocentric beliefs claiming that worshiping idols is a primitive act, and those who kneel before an inanimate object must believe that the object itself holds the divine power – an assumption that would render much of the world, as well as all of our Ancestors, congenitally unable to understand complex symbolism. For most people who do their devotions in front of a personal altar, however the objects on it are visual aids, memory aids. They attune the heart and mind to a certain reciprocity of practice, and help us open to the presence of our Gods because we are creatures of flesh, creatures dependent on sight and sound, taste and touch to interpret our world.

Symbols are the language of the spirit, the language that the Gods often choose to communicate with Their worshipers." (p. 152)

None of which denies that the Gods may use those objects and that space. An image may become enlivened, it may come to be infused with the energy of a Deity. The space – more and more as it is used – becomes holy space, with the very visceral sense of space and place that entails. These things are all part of the devotional equation. As you progress, try to be aware of when your mind, entrained by both monotheism and post-modern cultural elitism, is creating a roadblock: when you feel uncomfortable, when you are resistant to the process, when you are starting to feel superior to your ancestors. It happens – given the culture in which we're all raised, it would be surprising if it didn't at least once. Be aware of these times, note them, and then proceed anyway. In working with a shrine you are working with something *sacer*, a Latin word from which our world 'sacred' comes. It means not only 'to make sacred,' but more importantly 'belonging to the Gods.' You're entering into space you both share.

If you've never had a shrine before, the idea of creating one may seem at once both attractive and daunting. The best advice I can give really is: "just do it!" With the exception of specific taboos relevant to specific Deities, a shrine is a very personal expression of devotion. This is a good opportunity to begin developing the gift of discernment. Pray and meditate and feel it out. See what you are inspired to do. If you wonder whether something would be good on your altar, think about it. Reach out to the Gods and pray. And then listen and see what your 'gut' tells you. It's this internal sense that will be an invaluable guide toward interacting rightly and cleanly with the Gods, which is what, at its heart, devotional practice is.

I think shrines should be beautiful. They should reflect the devotion that you are building and tending and nurturing in your heart, a devotion that ideally overflows into every aspect of your life. This is all something that must be cultivated. (Remember that *cultus*, the devotional practice to a specific Deity, comes from a Latin word that also means 'to cultivate.'). An altar is in itself an offering, an ongoing one if it's tended regularly, so don't be afraid to start. Work from a desire to love and honor the Gods and be open to inspiration as it comes.

Suggestions:

I. If you don't have a personal shrine, either to your ancestors or Gods, consider creating one.

II. If you do have a personal shrine, redo it. Take everything off the shrine and rework it. Shrines are living things and they need consistent, tender loving care. I've found that the condition of one's shrine often mirrors the condition of one's spiritual connections so...keep it clean and active.

Actually, completely taking your shrine apart and redoing it from scratch is a really good thing to do every so often because it's easy to get caught up, both consciously and unconsciously, in preconceptions and to grow complacent and jaded. It's important that our devotional work be fresh. Taking down a shrine can be painful (I find it so), but it's good to take them down and reconstruct them from scratch every now and again. Think of it as spiritual spring cleaning. If you have never had a shrine before, then you have a really good opportunity facing you. Starting fresh forces you to actually learn the process. You don't, in such a circumstance, have the luxury of relying on a pre-established devotional tie. That's a good thing and something that should keep us all on our toes as we go.

Chapter 5:
Offerings

In this chapter, we're going to learn about libations, offerings, and basic respect. I've often said that there's one proper way to approach the Gods: respectfully. This desire to be in right relationship, the awareness that the Gods are real and holy powers, the awareness that They engage with us and the way that curbs and guides our behavior are all basic and essential building blocks of piety. I was reading an academic book on Roman religion recently and was struck by one of the comments in the text. On discussing animal sacrifice, the author wrote tersely (and accurately): "without butchery there is no piety." While we do not have to sacrifice animals (this is a very holy thing and not an everyday offering; it's also something that needs to be done by a specialist, a sacrificial priest or knife carrier), at the heart of this statement is the awareness that without offerings, without giving of ourselves and our resources, there is no piety. This is based around what historian Walter Burkert termed *do ut des* which comes from the Latin: "I give in order that you may give." In other words, it is through the establishment of a sacred reciprocity, giving and offering to the Gods, that we open the door to receiving Their blessings in return.

In Heathen circles one will often hear bitching, whining, and moaning: "Oh, you shouldn't give too much. The *Havamal* says that it's better not to give than to give too much," as the speaker is barely pouring out two drops of water. This is bullshit. Utter, unadulterated bullshit. Because: (a) that passage in the *Havamal* occurs in the section called the *Runatal,* where Odin wins the runes and specifically refers to negotiating with the rune spirits; and (b) if you're breathing you're not giving too much. With every breath we are further in debt to the Holy Powers and it is a debt we can never repay. It is not possible to give "too much" and even if it were, we're so far from that point in our communities that we don't have to worry. Worry instead about giving something well (within your means).

This is all part of the currency of devotion, the dynamics of gift exchange. Frankly, when people rail against making offerings I firmly believe that what they are, in fact, railing against is inconvenience. To keep the pathways of communication and commitment strong and flowing freely between you and your Gods, those roads must be paved with offerings of devotion. It is like fertilizing soil into which seeds have been planted, watering it and tending it with care so that those seeds will bloom.

I find it very uncomfortable to go to the Gods with empty hands (or the ancestors either for that matter). It just seems rude. I also think it's unhealthy to approach the Gods with such an attitude of want, or worse, penury: "I can't give. I won't have enough for myself. I need to hoard this for human use." Damn good thing the Gods don't feel that way! Entering into this reciprocal cycle nourishes us deeply and in ways that transform every aspect of our lives. Offerings don't have to be opulent. The most basic offering is clean water. I do not know of any Deity who will not accept this. If water is what you have to give, then it is an appropriate offering if given with a well-ordered heart. In fact, let me list some common types of offerings:

water   (This is *the* most basic offering. It's a good offering, a sacred one. If you have nothing else to give but you have water, then you have a good and proper offering.)
juice
alcohol
coffee/tea
sweets
prayer (special prayers in addition to regular praying, things like novenas, etc.)

hair   (Scandinavian bogs are full of long braids of hair that were cut off and offered. Short hair was shameful in many of these cultures, so if hair is all you really have to offer, and you wish to offer to the Gods, it makes a doubly powerful offering to cut it off.)

animals (which animal depends on the Deity)

tobacco

weapons

jewelry

fruits

cooked dishes

incense

flowers

good deeds, charitable donations, charity work

...and this list could go on and on.

What you give may be determined by finances and circumstances. There's no shame in giving only water if that is the best you have. In fact, for some Deities and ancestors, that is the desired offering. Conversely, if you are making a special offering outside of your regular devotions and prayers, you may wish to divine or have a skilled diviner do so to determine what offering is requested/required. I also do this after major rituals to determine how to dispose of the offerings that we've made and laid out.

For daily devotions, you won't need to do this. If you come to your shrine with a glass of wine or water and some flowers and make your prayers, there's no need to divine each time. Just dispose of the flowers when they wilt, and treat the food or drink left out as though it were the remains of a dinner party for an honored guest. Divination comes in to play for special rituals and special offerings. Let me give an example:

If I wanted to request a special boon from a Deity – say I was up for promotion but due to personality conflicts and inter-office politics, it looked like it would be a cold day in hell before I was given my promotion, and I wanted to request help of one of my Deities to make things fall into place – first, I'd divine and ask the

Deity in question if He or She was willing to intercede. If affirmative, I'd ask what offerings I should make. Then I'd ask how those offerings should be handled/disposed of. I'd leave nothing to chance. I'd also divine afterwards to make sure that the offering was acceptable and accepted.

It's a little different for daily devotions. The regular offerings you make bring you into closer communion with your Gods. They can be as simple or elaborate as you wish. I often pray but try not to let too many days go by before refreshing whatever offerings I've put on my shrines. The mindfulness itself is an offering too. I encourage folks to find what offerings you can make within your budget, simple things: a bit of incense, a glass of water along with your prayers. I had a colleague who would tell her students: "Don't be that person who only calls his family for bail money." In other words, don't only make offerings when there is a problem and you need help; make them a regular part of your devotional life and a way of saying thank you.

This is all a matter of hospitality. I often tell people who question the existence of the Gods (yet want to better their practice), "How would you behave and what would you do if you knew beyond a shadow of a doubt that the Gods were real and that They were listening or present?" Sometimes that conscious aware-ness makes all the difference. Be polite, be respectful. Understand that there is a hierarchy here and we are not at the top of the food chain. (If I seem a bit strident on this point, it comes of dealing with argument after argument in the communities in which I move, over why one should even give any offerings at all.) Make your offerings and make them a regular part of your practice.

One caveat: I do not think it wise to eat offerings. Once they've been made, that food or drink or whatever belongs to the Gods, not us. Again, it's rude and disrespectful to then eat it. There are some nuanced exceptions to this. Perhaps your Deity has pushed you to eat something once or twice. Perhaps this has evolved out of ongoing, lengthy practice. Perhaps divination has indicated that you should do this for your health or well-being. In these cases, I would do whatever your Deities wish, but in most cases I'd not touch an offering having been given. After all, what polite person gives a gift and then takes it back?

As I mentioned before, your offerings may be dictated to some degree by finances. Since this is a topic that often causes anxiety, it needs to be addressed in more detail here.

I am not poor. Several years ago I came into some money and this has transformed my life. I'm now able to go to school, live comfortably, and get proper medical care. Things were not always so, however. I spent the majority of my adult life, all of my twenties and most of my thirties, so poor that I still struggle with medical and dental problems caused by the level of poverty in which I lived. Those that say that poverty carries with it crushing psychological and emotional weight are correct. It does.

I've lived in sketchy neighborhoods in a one bedroom apartment with two and sometimes three roommates, struggling to make rent and survive. I've been homeless. I've stolen food in order to live. I still have anxiety about those times that comes back to me in nightmares whenever I am under any stress. When I talk about making offerings despite being poor, it's from my own experience.

Now, when I make offerings, I do my best to lay out a feast for the Gods. I don't ration, but get whatever I feel They want (and the ancestors too) and set it out. It's a joy, a tremendous joy to be able to do this because I remember times when I couldn't. For most of my devotional life, a candle and glass of water, prayers and time spent in contemplation before my shrine were all I had to give. Tending the shrine itself, even when it was bare-bones simple in its construction, was an offering. From any good food or sweets that I was given (it was usually possible to find food at work), part would be parceled out to the Gods. I would do things as devotional acts, and always there was prayer. I'm fortunate in that I can write, so writing prayers and poetry in offering, doing rituals were things that came naturally. But there were simple food and drink offerings too. Sometimes it was a teaspoon of food set aside from my own plate before I began to eat; sometimes it was a plate of whatever food I had cooked, when I had money for enough groceries to cook. Sometimes it was time. Sometimes a stick of incense broken into tiny parts to last for more days. Often it was just water, and keeping my altar clean.

I well remember the aching pain of wanting not only something better for myself, but the ability to give pretty things to the Gods, better things, better offerings. I've learned, though, not to rate offerings: if it's given from the heart, respectfully, then it suffices....but it must be given.

Poverty is no excuse. We're good at giving ourselves excuses and they're quite often, on the surface, logical excuses. Thing is, we can always find them if we try and in the end all they are is this: reasons not to do the most basic acts of devotion for our Gods, reasons not to do something that raises us up as human beings, reasons not to change, reasons not to do the very least that we can do. There's a time to put away excuses and instead take stock of what you are doing for your Gods and ancestors in your life. If you feel it is enough, then great. Keep at it. But if you see it lacking, if you feel you can do more, then maybe it's time to re-evaluate how, and when, and where. I think we can always do more: all of us. Not all offerings have to be tangible to be offerings, after all.

A Special Offering: Blót

For me as a Heathen, the two Solstices are times where, if I am able to do so, it is customary to make a sacrificial blót[1] to the Gods in thanks for all the blessings I and my house have received throughout the year. It is a time to gather with friends and co-religionists – those whose luck in some way is tied to mine – in order to make our offerings in joy, in reverence, and most of all in gratitude. A ritual like this is not something that is ever done lightly. It is perhaps the holiest rite we know. It is also one of the most anxiety-inducing, at least for me, because the responsibilities and sacred obligations for the one performing the blót and the

---

[1] Blót, which is pronounced to rhyme with 'boat,' is a ritual wherein offerings are given to the Gods. In some – not all – branches of Heathenry, this particular word is used, as I do here, only in reference to rituals where an animal is offered.

consequences to luck and wyrd for everyone involved should something go awry are immense.

Blót can be a terrible and terrifying thing – terrible in the older sense of the word: awe-inspiring, fear-inducing, and holy precisely because if done well, it places us directly in the sight of the Gods. It opens a door and creates a bond. It allows us to stand, for however long we engage in the rite, in that liminal space that begs and beckons to be filled with the presence of the Powers. It calls to Them with an urgency beyond the every day. Blót is a powerful point of connection, a tremendously sacred act. It's equally terrifying because of its very sacral nature. There is no room for error, no room for hesitation, no room for ego or anything else that might stand between the blótere[2] and the act of sacrifice. This, unlike any other ritual that we may choose to do, must be enacted with clean, uncompromising precision. Too much is at stake spiritually to do otherwise.

Leaving aside questions of whether or not the Gods want this type of sacrifice (obviously I believe They do, and certainly our lore attests to the fact that this was common amongst our ancestors, plus I have seen the blessings attendant on a well-executed blót and the bane that comes from one done disrespectfully), I am going to discuss the process of this ritual, specifically the internal process and preparation necessary to see it through successfully.

I have been a blótere for close to twenty years. I learned the technical skills first from diligent study and the assistance of a Santerian friend. Then later I was able to observe other blót priests in action during my time both with Ironwood Kindred and New Anglia Theod. The observation was almost as important as the actual training that preceded it.[3]

---

[2] Blótere is an Anglo-Saxon word for the priest who performs ritual sacrifices. On a tangential note, one of our most beloved goddesses, Freya, bears the title of 'blótere' for the Gods, which I personally find intriguing.

[3] Contrary to what I have seen claimed in various forums by members of New Anglia, I did not in fact learn how to perform a sacrificial blót from anyone in that Theod. I had been performing blót for my own kindred for many years before my association with New Anglia.

Blót is not a private thing. It is a community offering, a communal rite regardless of whether the sacrificed animal is given over completely to the Gods or shared in sacred feast amongst the folk. At its best it is a community experience of the holy. That being said, the act of slaughtering an animal is not one that most of us have seen close up. We do not live in a culture that has regular contact with every part of the cycle of preparing food for the table. Few of us raise and butcher our own livestock anymore. It can be an emotional shock to contemplate standing with a small group of people and consciously witnessing the killing of an animal. It doesn't matter that the killing is quick and painless — far more painless, I might add, then the way animals are commercially slaughtered in food production — it can still be quite an emotional shock. Therefore, I think it's important to see this act done in a respectful and sacred way. It helps immensely in finding the proper headspace when the time comes to make such an offering oneself.

Since I reached a point as a priest (and householder) where I could afford to make blót, I have tried to make some sort of sacrificial offering yearly at the two Solstices — especially at Yule, which I connect strongly to Odin. Regardless of my training and experience, I am terrified and often nervous and sick to my stomach each and every time I take up the sacrificial knife, utterly terrified. (Of course, I've learned over the years not to show that anxiety to the other attendees gathered, lest it make them equally uncomfortable.) It never changes and I think that's good. I think that anyone taking upon themselves the responsibility for making blót should be terrified. We should never get to the point where we can rest on our proverbial laurels. That way lies error and ultimately a bungled ritual, and if a blót is bungled not only might it negatively affect one's luck and wyrd, but an innocent animal might suffer and that, to my mind, is sacrilege. .

Doing a good blót isn't just a technical act. It's not just about making all the physical preparations, treating the animal well and ensuring a quick and painless kill, though those things are all very important. Over and above those necessary preparations, having the proper attitude is fundamental. I believe that humility, compassion, and most of all personal detachment are absolutely necessary for the blótere to be spiritually clean. There's no room for hesitation caused by nervousness or emotion. There's no room for that sentimentality which is really nothing more than ego or attention seeking couched as an emotional response. At the moment of sacrifice the blótere is the least important thing in the entire ritual. We are technicians and any personal emotional responses should be saved for later. Nothing, and I mean nothing can interfere with clean execution of one's sacral duty. In blót, that means nothing can interfere with getting oneself out of the way and making the requisite sacrifice cleanly and respectfully. No one should be focused on the priest and his or her emotional response to the matter at hand. The focus should be on offering the animal in question to the Gods and creating that moment of sacred connection. The focus should be on reaching out to the Powers.

I have a whole process that I go through before I actually step into the sacred space to perform a blót. Now this is my process and it works for me. At some point in their training (and I sincerely hope there is actually training), each blótere is going to have find his or her own way of getting into the proper, respectful frame of mind, and managing what can be the intensely strong emotions – both in oneself and one's fellow attendees – inherent in performing a blót. My preparations actually begin several days before the scheduled time of the ritual. I fast and cleanse via both cleansing baths and burning recels.[4] I will spend part of each day praying and meditating, preparing myself to enter into that detached headspace so necessary for me to function in this type of ritual. None of my own issues, fears, feelings, or anything else can be allowed to touch the moment of blót. Once I step into that sacred space and take up the ritual knife, I am there as a conduit, a vessel for the holy, a technician, and nothing of my human failings can be allowed to intrude. I must be absolutely and utterly clean. So for several days

---

[4] Anglo-Saxon medical/magical texts (there was little difference really) mention energetic cleansing via the burning of bundles of mugwort, so I often use mugwort in my preparations both of myself, my tools, and the space itself.

prior to the rite, I will meditate and also run through in my mind the technical process and structure of the ritual over and over again so I don't make any mistakes.

On the day of the rite, I take a cleansing bath and make sure that whatever I am wearing to the ritual is spotless. I do this out of respect for the Gods: that I not come before the Powers with poor hygiene! Then I spend more time praying and meditating, grounding and centering, and most importantly of all, I divine. I throw runes and take omens. I check and double-check that it is okay to do the blót, that I, the animal, and everything else is acceptable to the Gods. Before the ritual I bless my knife, I bless my garb, I bless my blót bowl. If it's there and about to be used in the rite, I'm probably blessing it. Of course I bless and pamper the animal too and thank it for its sacrifice.[5] I also divine on what should be done with the animal once it has been killed.

Now I've often been chastised for occasionally giving the entire sacrifice to the Gods, instead of butchering and cooking up the animal for the assembled folk after the rite. Sometimes, if divination (or a Deity directly) indicates during my preparations that such a thing is desired, I will place the carcass in a bonfire for total immolation (or, if a fire is not possible, bury it or place it at the base of one of my Godpoles). I do not assume that the animal will always be cooked and shared with the folk after the blót. Neither do I assume that it will always be given completely to the Gods. Often They are content with the life-force, the blood, and perhaps a portion of the meat. I always check, then double- and even triple-check beforehand (and sometimes after the blót has been performed as well).[6] I have been accused more than once of 'wasting' an

---

[5] Prior to the ritual itself, the animal, usually a small pig, is fêted. It's fed well and pampered, even coddled. It is treated like an honored guest. People may touch the pig, talk to it, give it milk, beer, fruit, ask it to convey messages to the other world, give it blessings. The sacrificial animal is treated like a king.

[6] Once, I was performing a blót to Odin in which we were preparing to sacrifice a young pig. Right as the pig was being led out to the Godpole, someone's gun went off. No one had touched the gun, it just went off. My

animal's life this way; however, let's remember that while blót may be a community ritual, first and foremost it is a gift to the Gods and the focus of the ritual should be on the Holy Powers and giving to Them, not on the community feast. That which is given to the Gods and ancestors is never wasted.

We as a people can be incredibly self-centered. Blót is a time to focus on the Holy Powers and if divination indicates that the Gods in question want the sacrifice given completely to Them, then that is the only thing that is right and proper to do. Good divination will tell the difference – and if one isn't prepared to acknowledge that the Gods may request what They want through various means large and small, then one shouldn't be doing blót. It's as simple as that. The Powers should drive the structure of blót, not our own comfort.

Which brings me to another point: the presence of the Gods can be very, very strong before, during, and even after a blót. It can lead to a sense of holy dread, of nervousness, or even outright terror amongst the gathered folk, particularly if they are sensitive to such things and have never experienced such intensity before. Tacitus mentions this sense of dread in his account of the rituals to Nerthus[7] and I myself have experienced it many times before and during blót. That sense of dread does not mean that anything is wrong. It means

---

colleague made sure everyone was unharmed, and then began to bring the pig forward. I immediately called for a halt, then called for my runes. After thorough divination, it became clear that the pig was not to be sacrificed. A devotee of Odin present was given the chance to take upon himself care of the pig (he owns a farm) as a votive animal for Odin. No blood was spilled that day, yet I consider it an excellent blót. I mention this here as an example of the type of spiritual receptivity needed to ensure a good blot – this is for the Gods. They should be central to the action, and therefore, the ones organizing and performing the rite should always be open to Their input. Skill in omen taking, to my mind, is essential for a skilled blótere. Also, not all Gods want this type of sacrifice. I would never offer an animal to Sigyn, for instance. It just would not seem appropriate. That's why divination is so important. Now not everyone has a talent for divination and that's okay. If the blótere isn't a skilled and confident diviner, there's no harm in calling in someone who has this talent.

[7] See Tacitus's *Germania*, chapters 40-42.

that we are about to encounter something very holy and holiness and terror all too often go hand in hand. A good blótere will prepare the people for this before the ritual space is even prepared. I often forget about this part, I have to admit. It never occurred to me that it would be an unusual experience for people (dealing with Odin for years has perhaps over-accustomed me to that sense of holy terror). But it is, and that needs to be addressed. We are dealing with Powers that are, for lack of a better word, inhuman, and there is often an ingrained fight or flight response to the sense of danger that can unconsciously evoke.

Blót is an oddity, really – a mixture of solemnity and joy. I think it's very, very important not to forget the joy. At its best, blót should be a celebration of the reciprocal connection that we share with our Elder Kin, the Holy Powers, the Gods and Goddesses that hopefully we both honor and love. That blend of solemn joy makes for a certain tension during the rite unlike any other ritual I have ever experienced. I think this is good. I think it's a sign of the importance and enormity of what we are doing when we decide to make a sacrificial blót.

So why do we do this? For love the Gods, for devotion, in reverence, and because it is the right thing to do. It is a sustaining act. It is not about killing an animal. It is not about shedding of blood. It is about acknowledging, celebrating, and renewing a very sacred contract between ourselves and the Powers. In all ways large and small, it is a celebration of the holy.

Chapter 6:
Clean and Clear

Now it is time to explore the important topics of discernment, signal clarity, cleansing, and miasma. As an aside, I tend to use the Greek term 'miasma' for any type of spiritual contamination (99% of the time, it is a neutral term: neither good nor bad, just a natural side effect of coming into contact with certain things). If you're up for some academic reading, I highly recommend R. Parker's book *Miasma: Pollution and Purification in Early Greek Religion* for a discussion of this type of contamination. We'll be touching on it in a bit below.

First I want to discuss signal clarity and discernment. In a way, these things go hand in hand. You'll often hear spiritworkers talk about 'signal clarity,' which is our fancy name for being able to clearly and accurately 'hear' (sense/interpret/etc.) the Gods and spirits. It's something many of us are obsessed with, because strong, clear signal clarity is absolutely necessary to do our work. Here's the thing though: a lay person might call that 'discernment.' They're not exactly the same thing. Not every lay person can actually hear the Gods or sense Them as strongly as a spiritworker, for whom signal clarity is an absolute must. There's *nothing* wrong with that. Discernment is the development of intuition and trust, of connection and communication with the Powers that leads to good judgment in putting our faith and devotion into action. It's a way of knowing that you have not erred from what your Gods may wish for you. You do not have to hear the Gods or sense Them strongly to have good discernment. Good discernment however is part of good signal clarity.

Discernment is the ability to accurately determine whether or not you have received a message clearly from your Gods, or whether you're listening to the sock puppets in your own head (or a negative spirit).

Catherine of Sienna, when being questioned on how she knew that she was actually talking to Jesus (and He back to her) said – and I'm paraphrasing here – that when "the devil" talks to you, the communication begins with sweetness and ends in misery and deception. When it is "God" it may begin with challenges, or difficulties but its end is always sweetness and truth.

I have found this to be so.

When we are listening to the imaginings of our own mind, our mental sock puppets, those sock puppets are usually reinforcing our areas of moral cowardice, weakness, indolence, poor character, laziness, co-dependence, egotism, etc....all those things that flee the occasional inconvenience of spiritual work. The Gods challenge us to be better.

Whether you have strong signal clarity or not, we all need discernment. "How do you know?" is the most common question that I'm asked as a god-servant, and that people ask each other and themselves when devotional experience is on the line. How do you know? The easy answer to someone deeply engaged is that you *know*. But that knowing, while some of us may not go into the nuts and bolts of it in conversation, is predicated on keeping our signal clarity clean and strong and on developing good discernment.

Discernment is best developed by doing the work of devotion – especially prayer. Praying often and well is one of the keys to the discernment practice. Face your fears. They are the biggest blocks to good discernment. Work through your issues, do not allow yourself the easy out of an excuse. Doing that consistently will bring up all of the issues, fissures, and 'crap' that you can then deal with. This type of internal work is not devotion. It's the prerequisite and ongoing requirement of devotion. I believe this is why one of the precepts at the oracle of Delphi was "Know thyself." That's an ongoing thing and it takes ongoing work. Yes it is difficult and there's not much in our culture that encourages such work, but the difficulty is irrelevant. It must be done. The biggest thing we can all do to develop good discernment is to stop giving ourselves excuses and outs as to why we can't do what we know the Gods require.

In addition to poor discernment, there are other things that can impact signal clarity too (and signal clarity – inasmuch as each person is able to develop it – is a grace and blessing of spiritual work) and one of those things is miasma.

Miasma is contamination of some sort: spiritual, physical, psychological, emotional. At its harshest and worst it renders you unfit to be in the presence of the Gods, but usually it blocks signal clarity. I want reemphasize that miasma is a morally neutral thing. In ancient Greece, one could enter into a state of miasma, for instance, by attending a wedding. Miasma is a neutral contagion that affects a person in such a way that they may not be functioning in the best, most optimal way spiritually. Left untended it can really muck up one's signal clarity. If it is emotional or psychological, it may impact one's ability to have any type of discernment at all.

It is on us to remain free of miasma and to deal with it when it occurs, which can happen naturally in the course of our day. This is why cleansing is so important. More than anything else, I think that it is staying spiritually and energetically clean that contributes to good, clear, accurate signal clarity and discernment. It's also the piece of the puzzle that is most often neglected. We forget. We get busy. We procrastinate. This is normal, but with this particular thing it's best to make it a regular part of your practice: cleanse, cleanse, cleanse. It really is, as the saying goes, next to godliness!

My friend Sophie reminded me awhile back of a quote supposedly by Aleister Crowley: "Cleanliness is next to godliness and by god had better come first!" This is why all those spiritual/ energetic cleansings are so important. Try to make a habit of doing one at least once a week. We pick up an awful lot of psychic gunk just going about our day. Questions of miasma and signal clarity aside, that shit – I'll call it what it is – can make you sick. Cleansing regularly is a good habit to develop.

I don't think we talk enough about how to handle miasma, what it is, and why it's important to be mindful about it, and this is something crucial to clean spiritual practice. I'll take that a step further: I don't think the concept of miasma is covered at all in Western mystery traditions/esotericism, nor have I seen it much openly discussed in polytheist circles. I think lots of us know how to handle it personally, but I really think it's important to discuss this across communities. There's a Lukumi saying that when an elder dies and entire world dies with him (or her) and that is so true. We need to pass this information on, spread it about, get it out there so that our communities themselves become living libraries. For those coming into the traditions this would be a godsend, and for us a boon.

I think the biggest stumbling block that I see some folks having around this whole idea is language. I tend to use 'miasma' as a catch-all for any type of spiritual contamination. I avoid the word 'impurity' like the plague unless I'm dealing with folks with whom I've worked for years, or whom I've trained. The reason for this is that such a word can be very triggering. I've seen people really hit a wall with this. It becomes difficult to really grasp at a gut and bone level that with miasma, with this type of impurity, there's no moral judgment in most cases. It's a natural consequence. For instance, I attend a wedding, I have gone into a state of miasma. I help prepare a relative's body for cremation (which I did with my dad), and I am in miasma. It doesn't matter that I've done something proper, the 'contagion' or 'contamination' is a natural side effect. It's not a matter of repression or moral judgment. So I try hard to use neutral language. Of course one can fall into impurity or miasma by neglecting the internal work so necessary to spiritual practice, or by blaspheming, or doing something morally wrong, but even there while the action that causes the miasma in these cases may be wrong or at least ill thought out, the miasma itself is a neutral thing.

In July 2014, my partner Sannion posted several questions about miasma to his blog, inviting people from across various polytheistic communities to answer. I'm going to share both his questions and my answers here, because they're worth considering. I know simply working my way through his questions caused me to seriously think about how I handled miasma, and to correct certain bad habits I'd been neglecting.

"Does your tradition recognize pollution and how is it handled?"

I actually haven't heard it much discussed in Heathenry, which is unfortunate. We have a concept of fire consecrating and purifying and of marking off sacred space but I haven't come across anything in the surviving sources specifically related to miasma. There are hints, particular in some of the Anglo-Saxon herb charms and one can easily extrapolate that while it may not have been called 'miasma,' that there was the idea of spiritual contagion. Mugwort or even the nine herbs charm is noted as being used for clearing this type of thing.

I hadn't given it much thought myself in practice until I helped prepare my father's body for cremation. It was a holy thing, the proper thing to do but midway through I became intensely aware of the miasma on me. From that day on, I started paying attention. (This also drove home the fact that miasma is *not* 'sin.' I think that's where a lot of folks get hung up. It's not sin and there's no moral judgment on most types of miasma.

"Is pollution only relevant in certain circumstances (i.e., when entering sacred space and dealing with certain gods) or is it something that needs to be dealt with across the board, including in our regular, daily lives?"

Personally, I really think it's something we should be mindful of in our regular, daily lives. Pollution is one of the things that can dramatically impact and block one's signal clarity and spiritual discernment. It blocks us off from clear communication with the Gods and can, I believe, leave us open to spiritual and psychic ills. (Think of what would happen physically if you didn't ever bathe for instance. It's the same sort of thing.)

In many respects, miasma is inevitable. This is why technology existed amongst our polytheistic ancestors for cleansing it away. If the regular cleansings aren't enough, then there's divination to figure out what needs to be done, but I've found that regular attention to this goes a long way

"What ritual technology does your tradition have for dealing with this and what do you think someone just starting out should do and know about this?"

We have a number of herbal combinations and charms recounted in some of our lore for using smoke to cleanse. There's also purification by sacred fire (I've used this myself, adapting it to use modern hand lamps to run fire around myself safely). Living with a Dionysian as I do, I've learned a few other things too, like the application of *khernips.* I also think that while a lot of our sacred lore and practices may not have been recorded, we can find an awful lot of information in folklore. I have a fair knowledge of conjure work, and some of the charms and practices seem to me to be specifically focused around keeping clean and ridding oneself of malign influences. This is something that can be adapted.

For me, I do regular cleansings as part of my work and I keep a strong eye on myself so I am aware of when I fall into miasma – and really, when we are crossing the boundary between the sacred and profane, this is inevitable. It's something to deal with as a matter of course, like washing your hands before dinner. I make liberal use of *khernips* before and after rituals and fire cleansings too. I think part of the practice of consecrating a space with fire blessing that is drawn from Anglo-Saxon lore involves consciously ridding what will be ritual space from any miasma.

"Is pollution physical or strictly spiritual? Is this even a useful dichotomy to entertain?"

I think with the case of miasma, it can occur on either level or both. I don't maintain much dichotomy here – I'd be curious as to how others might answer this question. I do the physical cleansings, with often include a spiritual component and have never parsed it out beyond that. I think that we are physical creatures so there's always a physical component, an interface to what we do.

"What are some of the consequences of paying too little or too much attention to it?"

I think it can open a person up to spiritual, psychic, and sometimes physical illness. It cuts us off from clean communication with the holy. It impacts signal clarity and discernment. It can damage our luck and worst of all we become a carrier for the contagion, because that's something I haven't heard discussed too often: miasma is contagious.

Following this round of questions, which at the time, I posted on my blog, a reader asked a couple of really insightful follow up questions:

"Two questions! First one: as someone who tends to suffer from anxiety, how should I approach cleansing? I run a big risk of getting too anxious about miasma – a catch-22 because anxiety seems to accrue it, in my experience at least. So my cleansings will start to not work, or I'll get burnt out from overdoing them, and the miasma will be the same as it was before (if not worse).

I suspect the answer lies in holding to the same ritual, having faith that it will work. I worry about practitioners who have OCD, though.

Second question: can you talk a little more about how miasma is contagious?"

Those are both really good questions. Firstly, there is no need to become overly obsessed with cleansing. If you have a structure in place that you perform regularly (before attending any shrines for instance) then you should be fine for most things (exceptions like oh, say, Oedipus, are outside my pay grade!). It's wise to be aware of miasma, but regular, consistent maintenance is usually all that's required. Miasma is a natural thing and I think that because of that, there are some very simple ways to tend to it. Effectively, it's going to happen. You will pick up miasma. It's unavoidable because it is a natural byproduct of certain places and things. I tell people don't stress, just be mindful. Really understanding that 90% of miasma is a perfectly natural by-product of a thing, for me at least, helps immensely in keeping me from obsessing about it.

I have found that anxiety does increase miasma...it opens you up and makes you vulnerable to a lot of negative energy (including that generated by yourself). This is one of the reasons that I recommend consistent (as in daily) grounding and centering. Usually ten minutes in the morning and ten in the evening will suffice. In theory, I try to keep my home clean and uncluttered but it's a work in progress.

I recommend the following in general: have a cleansing regimen (and it doesn't have to be severe) that you perform before praying or attending any shrines. (If you are a diviner, have the same sort of thing before and after clients.) This can be as simple as washing hands and aspersing head with *khernips*. Once a week I do a serious cleansing (usually meditation, cleansing bath, smoking with certain herbs, *khernips*, and other sorts of purification following up with divination), usually at week's end because let's face it, even aside from miasma, we pick up a lot of psychic shit just going about our day. I don't much worry about it beyond that. If you're doing the regular purifications before prayers, and you're praying regularly you should be fine for most things.

I also recommend seeing a diviner at least twice a year (preferably every three months) to make sure that everything is in order and balance spiritually. If there are any ongoing issues with miasma it will come up there.

I also think that there's internal and external miasma. If you're doing the personal work necessary for cleanly engaged spirituality, then that goes a long way toward limiting internal miasma...which I find far worse than external because it can affect our emotions (or even arise from unaddressed issues, denial, resistance to evolving spiritually) and is incredibly tenacious and difficult to remove (because I think we unconsciously hold onto it). This is one of the reasons why all the challenging internal work is so important.

I do believe that internal miasma can be contagious at times, but external miasma is particularly so. Think about it like regular, physical dirt: if you brush up against someone who is covered with dirt, you're likely to get dirty too. Or think of it as the spiritual equivalent of the common cold. I have seen people so riddled with miasma internal and external that there was just no way they weren't contaminating everything around them. I avoid these people. In fact, I tend to instinctually avoid anyone deeply miasmic, something that has caused problems with students in the past (since part of the learning process is dealing with buried issues, dredging that up, and working it out, there's usually a point where students become deeply miasmic). I also think that sometimes internal miasma happens because we've exposed ourselves to a person or a thing that has put us in a headspace where we are vulnerable to it.

This is partly why I am so incredibly careful about with whom I share ritual space. Miasma spreads. If I walk through a field of *Xanthium*, I'm going to come out with burs stuck to my pants. If I enter a space with people who are miasmic, the cleaner I am going in, the less miasma I pick up but I'm still going to have to cleanse when I come out.

I also think certain types of miasma can attract negativity, but it has to be significant and untended for this to be the case. Mostly, it impairs and impedes one's relationship with the Gods, which is reason enough in my book to deal with it!

To give you a further idea of how miasma may work, I want to share something that happened to me recently. The following was originally written on August 1, 2014:

> Today is the feast of Dionysian kings and I was really looking forward to participating in ritual with my partner, the Archiboukolos of the Thiasos of the Starry Bull. There are several of the honored dead within this group that I particularly venerate and I had offerings and such all planned. That I am currently sitting well outside of any ritual space typing this instead of participating in sacred rites is in part the subject of this post. Until about fifteen minutes ago when I finished the first round of cleansing work, I was massively riddled with miasma. There was no way I could enter sacred space.
>
> It started two days ago. Several of my friends just got back from a trip to Poland. One of them, a very, very close

friend knows that as a vitki and shaman I collect dirt and stones from various places. It's a way that I am able to establish connections with a plethora of land and city spirits. Quite often when she travels, my friend brings me back a bit of soil here, a stone there, and anything else that she thinks I may like and find useful in my work. She's very intuitive and knows enough to trust her gut and she respects the work I do (as I respect her). So we were having breakfast on Thursday, the day after she got back, and after giving me some pretty cards, an icon (of my favorite image of Mary – the black Virgin of Czestochowa), jam, a little sculpture, and a gorgeous art photograph, she pulled two baggies out of her loot-bag. "I brought you dirt," she said, dropping the first one into my hands.

Now I knew she'd spent the better part of her visit in Krakow so I immediately responded, "Oh, is this from Krakow....." and stopped because as soon as I had it in my hands I knew it wasn't. She shook her head, watching to make sure I was okay and said, "No, it's from Auschwitz-Birkenau." Then as I quickly set the bag down, she gave me the second one, which was from a lovely little town about half a day's ride outside of Krakow. I wrapped the soil up and put it carefully away, purposely blocking it from my thoughts. When I brought it home, I put it haphazardly on my ancestor-table, asking them to lock it down until I figured out what to do with it (memorial work, prayer, elevations most likely). I forgot apparently to tell my partner that I had it, and went about my day. I was at a bit of a loss as to how best to deal with it – it was unlike anything I'd touched before – and figured I'd tend to it in a bit after I'd thought about it awhile. It is a powerful gift but one that requires respectful handling.

I was really tired by the end of the day Thursday and had some ritual obligations so I didn't get a chance to do anything about it. Today, I woke up and hit the ground running dealing with a dozen other things. I was feeling really 'off,' uncomfortable, kept thinking that I smelled off (I had bathed and was fine but energy often translates as scent to me), felt very, very tired and just filthy. By the time Sannion and I went out to get a few last minute offerings, I told him that I didn't think I could participate tonight in the ritual, I was feeling too unclean. By the time I got home, I was feeling really sick and feverish with an upset stomach (also a common side effect when I'm miasmic) so I sort of passed out on the sofa for an hour or so.

A friend and colleague came over to drop off some statuary and I woke up and we started chatting and I mentioned feeling ill and miasmic and couldn't figure out why. A little later I mentioned my friend's gift. I've never quite seen a look of horror like the one that flitted across my colleague's face. I'm sure it was matched only by my own when I had the bag of dirt initially dropped into my hands. This was the first my partner had heard of it too and we all realized exactly why I was feeling so filthy and ill. My colleague left and I immediately did divination and figured out how to best and respectfully contain the soil (wrapped in silk, then wrapped in more silk, then put in a pretty pouch, then in a box filled with tobacco leaves – tobacco consecrates – into which prayers had been given and several prayer cards carefully put). I made offerings and secured the box between two sacred objects deep in the bowels of my ancestor shrine, then I went upstairs to do the cleansing bath of all cleansing baths. There was salt, dragonsblood soap, the entire bath was made of *khernips*, rose water, and a few special ingredients from my Odin shrine. I even scrubbed down with blessed salt scrub that I have, in addition to the salt in the water. Got out, put on clean clothes, covered my head with a special headwrap and now I'm here typing this before I go up to do more ritual work. I may even dig out my white clothes that I use for Orisha stuff and spend the next few days all in white – white is a very energetically sterile color. I'll also be doing quite a bit of prayer and ritual within the hour. Yes, the taint was that bad.

Things that happen leave residue in the land and that doesn't just go away, especially things of such horrific magnitude. I have no idea how that land could ever be cleansed. If I had my way, that and places like it would be open memorials where people could go to make offerings, elevations, and constant prayer. One of the things that I've decided to do, as a result of this unexpected miasma, is to put together and emergency cleansing kit. I keep a full first aid kit in my home and it seems logical given the work that I do, to keep a similar kit for spiritual emergencies like this.

This is something good and practical that I'd not ever considered before that's come out of this and that is a gift and I consider it an unexpected gift from my friend. It's something that will serve me well for a very long time to come. I also realize that I need to be much, much more mindful in the land work that I do and how I communicate that to my friends. I had been concerned when my friend told me she was visiting Auschwitz and had urged her to cleanse before and after but I myself hadn't done any of that upon handling the soil. I know better and while I can get away with cutting some corners in my work (I'm experienced and I know a few short cuts), this isn't one of them. It was a good lesson. This is yet again a reminder of why having an established protocol for one's devotional work, spiritual work, and esoteric work in general is oh so necessary. I won't be forgetting again anytime soon.

In the meantime, here are some preliminary thoughts on what I'm going to be putting in my cleansing kit:

* dragonsblood soap
* florida water
* himalayan salt
* mugwort recaning sticks
* bay leaves

* candle and lighter
* set of whites
* rose water
* stones: hematite, black tourmaline, tiger iron, etc.
* a cologne for cleansing
* Sandalo 1800 colonia
* salt scrub
* white kaolin clay
* head wrap
* prayer cards
* silk scarves (for wrapping shit up in – fake silk works pretty much as well as the real thing)
* tobacco
* self-lighting charcoals and a good cleansing incense
* my favorite perfume – scent is a powerful thing for me and I often use it to transition back to mundane headspace after Work. Certain scents make me feel better in my skin.
* divination travel kit.
* travel shrine (I make them about the size of an Altoids box so they *are* travel shrines)

My friend did everything right. She brought me an amazing gift. She'd hinted that she would bring me dirt from Auschwitz. I had totally forgotten by the time she did -- I've been frenetically busy and it was one of the mental balls I inadvertently dropped. The only error here was mine.

We all get in over our heads at points, or have questions that we ourselves cannot answer even with the best discernment in the world. That's when you go to a diviner or seek out an oracle. Your diviners are there to help sort out those questions that you can't tend yourself, and to provide regular insight into whether or not you're walking your path rightly and well. I often recommend seeing a good diviner at least every three months. It's a way of making sure that you are staying on the right course for yourself and your Gods and heading off any problems, or better preparing yourself to deal with them.

I generally don't recommend doing divination for yourself if you are deeply concerned or emotionally connected to an issue. If your signal clarity and discernment are both already compromised by anxiety or fear, then how on earth can you possibly read accurately? You need someone objective and a good diviner is precisely that.

One other way that you can double-check your discernment and signal clarity is, when the situation is an especially important one, to ask for an omen. Pray and tell your Gods that you're concerned that you may not have the best signal clarity and you mean no disrespect but you want to get this right and so could they send you a sign in the world around you. Then pay attention. I've seen it come via animals showing up, via billboards, even passing trucks. (No joke. I was once wondering which Deity wanted to be honored at a ritual and divination was inconclusive so I asked for a sign. Ten minutes later I went outside to smoke and a truck with the word "Hela" passed by. Hela is the Norse Goddess of the underworld. Message received!) If it sounds silly, keep in mind that: (a) it was common in the ancient world to consider omens; and (b) the Gods will communicate with us through that which is around us. I don't do this a lot and I don't recommend doing it overmuch. We want to develop discernment and signal clarity and an ability to communicate, not rely over much on omens and divination but there is a time and place for everything.

Mostly I want to point out that developing discernment and better signal clarity, like devotional life in and of itself, takes care. It takes attention. It takes tending. As with devotion itself, the work will teach you how to do it. Discernment develops as trust and communication with the Gods develops and prayer is your primary tool there. Some of this is a development of personal discipline: avoid those things and people that do not enhance your relationship with the Gods. Seek out those that do. This is part of the process of reprioritizing and centering your life around your devotional world. Simply cull those things that do not enhance that – something easier said than done in many respects. It's a process of constant evaluation and re-evaluation, and always there is the going back to your shrine to the Gods in prayer and meditation and that is how discernment is developed.

Ritual is one of the ways that one can engage in devotional practice. Ritual may be parsed into several categories: public/private, large/small/solitary, formal/informal. Each one takes a specific skill set and while there is nothing wrong with leading ritual for yourself, facilitating it as a priest/ess or leading for others requires both experience and training (something largely lacking in our communities as a whole). There is a skill set inherent in a well-structured, well-run ritual and likewise a different skill set is required for huge group rituals versus smaller group rituals. I'm not going to be discussing huge 200+ group rituals here. That's well beyond the scope of this chapter and largely irrelevant to the scope of this book. Instead, we're going to be talking about personal rituals and by extension small group rituals. While there are differences, sometimes significant, between these latter two types of ritual, the basic structure that one would effectively follow is largely the same. From there, it is a matter of adapting for personal or small group use.

So what is a ritual? Wikipedia would doubtless say that any repetitive action done with intent is a ritual but I think that's a bit facile, and waters down the word beyond usefulness. I'm going to stick solidly in the realm of theology and ritual studies here in my definitions. At its core, it's a structured way of engaging with the sacred. It's a container for such engagement to happen. It's a protocol by which we can maintain right relationship in our direct engagements with the sacred. It's part of the dance of devotion.

A well-constructed ritual has three parts: the beginning, where one transitions into sacred space, the middle, where engagement happens, and the end, where one transitions back into regular space. In ritual studies there is the concept of *kronos* versus *kairos*: regular time versus ritual time, or more literally, the right time. When you are doing a ritual, you're stepping out of regular time and into liminality. A ritual is a container where this alchemy of the devotional dance may more directly occur. A good ritual facilitates, first and foremost, not only engagement with the Holy but the receptivity and vulnerability of head and heart space that makes that possible. Regular rituals bracket our day, our week, our month, our year with excursions into the realm of the sacred. A good ritual leader knows how to create the container (i.e., sacred space), guide others into that space in a way that allows for receptivity to the Gods and spirits, and bring everyone safely back again (and get them grounded and centered afterwards). He or she is responsible for holding the space, and monitoring every person in the ritual, seeing that they manage the necessary transitions well, always making room in whatever structure there is, for the Gods and ancestors to flow in and intervene.

Understanding that there is a flow and a process, a structure to the ritual process is crucial. This is so even if you are doing rituals only for yourself (by 'only' I do not in any way dismiss personal rituals. In fact, I think that they are absolutely crucial. We may join with others in ritual to venerate and celebrate the Powers but the real work of devotion and spirituality occurs alone, in the secret fastness of our hearts, when we're pouring ourselves out in private devotion and rituals by ourselves with only our Gods and spirits). I've often said that a good ritual is like a good essay: it has a beginning, a middle, and an end, and everything refers in some way back to the main thesis! This does not mean, of course, that rituals have to be complex. In fact, I've found the most powerful rites are often those that are the simplest. You want to keep it to the point, and avoid throwing in everything including the kitchen sink.

Now there are lots of tools that we can incorporate in ritual work, but they are just tools. They don't make the ritual. These include chanting, dancing, prayer, incense, music, other types of sound, etc. Using incense or meditating isn't something that belongs to any one faith. These are tools that may be used and adapted and that have been used and adapted by nearly every tradition I can think of in some way or another, with varying emphasis. Don't get hung up on the tools and ephemera.

In scrolling through the various blogs that I generally read as a matter of course, I came across a comment (from a non-theistic pagan of course) asserting that the primary purpose of ritual was "to experience a sense of community." Of course I disagree, as I suspect would many of my polytheistic colleagues but since ritual can surely provide a sense of community feeling, I wanted to clarify why I found the statement troubling. I'm not going to go into a discussion of what ritual is, or how to construct one, or what its constituent parts might be though I have the formal training in ritual studies to do so. It's not important to this discussion. Instead, I'm going to focus on what, to a devotional polytheist, the purpose of ritual might be. Then, I'm going to share a brief outline of a typical House Sankofa ritual to give you some idea of what I get up to in my community ritual work.

Firstly, that a ritual can bring about a sense of community is a side effect. It's not the purpose of a ritual. To stop there is like stopping a six course dinner before reaching the main course. It's a by-product, nothing more, of a well-run public ritual. (I specify public, because there are individual and personal rituals as well that do not involve any other members of one's community). Of course it is a joy and a comfort to find oneself in the presence of like-minded folks, all the more so when you're all collectively paying homage to the holy. This goes without saying. It is not, however, the purpose of a ritual, not to a polytheist. You see, this comes down again to where one puts the locus of one's devotional focus: on the self (non-theistic pagans) or on the Gods (polytheists). While there are rituals that can bring a tremendous amount of healing to all involved, I've never been a fan of ritual as therapy, ritual as self-help, ritual as entertainment, or ritual as social club. I would like to think that as a species we're not that self-absorbed. Clearly though, I'm an optimist.

There are rituals where the focus of the ritual is the transition of a person from one state of being to another. Coming of age ceremonies are a perfect example. I would personally not call such services 'ritual,' but might refer to them as 'ceremonies' instead, though this is parsing semiotics at this point. Suffice it to say that when I talk about ritual here, I'm referring to a basic ritual in which the Holy Powers are in some way invoked. The word itself comes from Latin and refers specifically to religious customs and sacred rites. Durkheim be damned, those of us who actually honor the Gods believe that there is more to religion than social mummery.

For a devotional polytheist, the purpose, first and foremost, of a ritual is paying homage to, honoring, and expressing veneration for the Holy Powers (Gods and/or ancestors). That it can be done in a community or at least group setting lends power to the rite and is in itself a joy. Ideally, one's religious expression in ritual is the culmination of all the devotion and practices that one has engaged in by oneself. Throughout, the point of one's attention and mindfulness is on the Powers.

When someone asks me how to create a ritual, that is what I tell them: everything you do or say should in some way honor the Holy Powers. Social hour can come after the ritual, during potluck. I once had a colleague tell me about a ritual she attended where the facilitator stopped in the middle to chat with a friend about how much she wanted to travel to London. I've seen people complain when rituals took more than 10 or 15 minutes and when they weren't allowed a share in the offerings given to the Gods and/or dead. I've seen interfaith rituals where no specific Holy Powers were ever once invoked. I once saw a woman start filing her nails during an invocation. To all of this, I say no. that is not appropriate ritual behavior. Save it for social hour, folks. From the moment the space is consecrated and ritual begins, the focus is on the Gods and/or ancestors.

It's for this reason that while I've seen, participated in, and even led lovely rituals that incorporated activities, meditations, ritual drama, etc., in the past, more and more I'm coming to favor simple offertory rites. I wouldn't necessarily exclude those other tools and techniques, because they can be quite powerful and effective, but when it comes to teaching people that stepping into ritual space carries with it a necessary corollary of turning one's mind and attention firmly on the Gods, I find that the simpler rites are best. There is still beauty and there is still drama, but it's much easier for a newcomer to see where the appropriate focal point might be.

To highlight what I mean here, I want to share an outline of a basic House Sankofa ritual. This is a format that we generally adapt as needed. Sometimes we get more elaborate, sometimes less but this structure has served us well, blended House that we are.

Preparation for ritual usually starts one week, sometimes two (occasionally more) before the actual day of the ritual itself. The night before, the space will be thoroughly cleaned physically and energetically. An altar will be set up, usually on the floor. Sometimes we raise them up and use an altar table, but our House tends to follow the custom of setting up the altars on the floor. We usually don't complete the altar the night before. An altar is an invocation, a living welcome to the Deities involved, so we complete that welcome right before the ritual when the last items and offerings will be placed. Divination is done to confirm that so far, everything is pleasing to the Powers involved and that no different or further offerings than what has been planned are desired.

People usually start gathering an hour before ritual. I usually ask that folks bring whatever they wish to offer (I almost always provide a list of appropriate and/or traditional offerings a week or so before the rite) and something for potluck. Offerings are organized and placed where they need to be. We might talk a little bit about the Deity or Deities behind honored, and if there's anything that people want to add to the altar, they do so at this time. In many cases, I will divine again to make sure that what we are doing is pleasing to the Deity or Deities in question, that nothing more is needed, and that we are good to proceed.

Before we start I, or whoever is leading, will go over the order of the rite, what is going to happen, when, and what people can expect. If there are any taboos associated with the God or Gods being honored they are shared with those gathered then. Then I call folks into the space and begin by consecrating the space. We have now entered ritual time and space:

* An offering is given to the Powers that guard the roads of both blessing and misfortune.
* Offerings are given to the ancestors along with prayers.
* The Deity or Deities being honored are invoked. Many prayers are given by various folks in attendance honoring Them.
* Offerings are made.
* Usually there is a chant or galdr or something and during this time, people may go up to the altar and make personal petitions, prayers, speak private words before the image of the Gods, etc. The chant honors the Deities but also creates interference so that no one else can hear what each devotee might be saying to the Powers.
* More offerings are made. If there is anything special going on in this particular ritual, it usually happens here.
* If it is a Norse ritual, a horn might be passed.
* At this point there is usually either another long prayer, or a call and response.
* Special petitions may be made.
* The Gods and ancestors are thanked.

Then we close ritual space and move into another room for potluck and socializing. Some people usually want to spend more time by the altar communing with the Gods and they are free to do so. I or another diviner in the House will then do divination to make sure that the ritual was acceptable, the offerings were acceptable, and that it is right and proper to conclude the rite. Our rituals take about an hour and a half to two hours usually from start to finish. Ancestor rituals tend to run a bit longer. There are exceptions to this order of ceremony and what I've described here is a generic structure, a flexible structure that we often alter to accommodate various Deities or as need dictates.

For personal rituals, how does all this translate? Well, prepare yourself well. Give yourself markers that help you transition from *kronos* to *kairos*. Magicians have raised this type of thing to a high art. That's why there are special garments, and incenses, and oils, and preparatory work....it's less about the ritual in many cases, than about getting the practitioner in the proper headspace *for* the ritual! I would say meditate, set up, cleanse yourself. Then make sure you won't be disturbed (turn off the phone) and then begin your rite. Mindfulness is the key, whether you're doing a public/group ritual or a private one. When you're done, pay just as much attention to your transition back to *kronos*. So much of good ritual is about managing transitions.

Now don't think that rituals have to be formal. Most of my personal ones are really, really not. What they all have in common is that mindful structure: transition in, engagement, transition out. All the order, aesthetics, and drama in the world can be involved but if we're not centered and mindful in our purpose, then the ritual isn't a ritual. What is necessary is a common focus: i.e., engagement with and veneration of the Powers too. In ritual, we're stepping into liminal space. It's a magical thing and all those tools I mention above, bringing the sensorium (sight, smell, sound, taste, touch) into the process helps further the necessary transitions. There should be a reason for everything you include in ritual and that is a valid one: it increases attunement to the holy.

(I'll let you in on a secret: I detest traditional Heathen ritual style. I think it's largely a crock. There's no historical evidence for symbel as we do it (blot, yes, symbel no) and they're boring. Being so strongly influenced by Protestant ideals, they aim to strip away anything mystical, sensual, experiential, and are structured to serve the community not the Gods, and in fact to keep the Gods at bay. Consistent, effective ritual work makes one more sensitive to the energy of the Divine presence and I think this may be one of the reasons – a community discomfort with the Gods – that Heathen ritual is so incredibly ineffective. There can be deep community ambivalence toward engaging with the Holy and a dogged insistence that engagement is occurring when really the focus is on anything but.)

Doing ritual makes you more sensitive to the Gods. It's a discipline, a practice even if all you're doing is one ritual a month. Start where you start. You're stepping into liminal space and placing yourself before the Gods in a very direct and vulnerable way. It is a tremendous act of courage sometimes.

Where to start: (1) Have a clear purpose in mind (i.e., I want to honor Deity X). (2) How often in your week do you feel the need to give time for a ritual? Try to be consistent. Your practice will evolve as you do, but consistency is a good discipline to encourage. Seeds take time to root themselves and grow after all. Consistent practice is like sunlight, warming the earth, giving nutrients, and encouraging those seeds to grow. It's necessary. (3) Give yourself time for transitioning into and out of ritual headspace.

The pitfall of doing ritual work is that it can become rote. Alone it can, for some people, be more problematic and difficult getting into deep devotional or ecstatic headspace. There can be a tendency to fixate on details to the detriment of what you actually want to do. You can lose sight of the meaning of the rite, or struggle with signal clarity. As with prayer, the key is to just keep on keeping on and to address the internal work, the hard emotional stuff, as it comes up. Don't run from yourself. That to my mind is one of the maxims of good devotional work. Keep as clean energetically as possible. I also find it helpful to keep a journal, as I suggested at the beginning of this book. I still have all my journals from my very first year of work and I refer back to them (sometimes, I'll admit, with embarrassment).

Try to go into your rituals without any preconceived notions or expectations. They'll block the Gods and kill the experience. When I was first called by the Norse Gods, it was largely Loki Who came calling and He led me to Odin. For many years, They refused to allow me to join a kindred, or associate with the Heathen community, or even read much of the lore (beyond the basic Eddic tales). Eventually that was lifted and I was expected to familiarize myself with the relevant material and pushed (bitching and moaning all the way) into the community but this only happened once I had a solid relationship with the attendant trust already established. The reason? Had I gone to Odin and Loki with any preconceptions, even subconsciously, it would have been damaging and would have prevented me in so many ways from developing a good, clean, healthy devotional relationship with Them. I'm still, to this day, eminently grateful for that early taboo! The Gods are opportunists and will use the avenues we give Them for communication but I think it's best if we don't complicate matters for ourselves. An awful lot of damage and atrophy can be done to one's spiritual and devotional life by clinging to preconceptions. Try to jettison them early, often, and well.

Many years ago, my Kindred developed a morning and evening rite that we each did daily (sometimes together, as at that point half of us lived in the same neighborhood). It can be helpful to have personal rituals for rising and sleeping, centering your day on the Gods. They can be as elaborate or simple as you wish. I encourage folks to work on creating these for yourself. For instance, in working with Iris, I've begun a small ritual in the morning before I leave for work: I cleanse and dress, asperse with *khernips* and offer a prayer to Her. I spend a few moments – not more than five as this is a quick morning ritual – opening up to Her presence and blessings, give thanks, light a bit of incense, etc. When I'm done, I ring a bell (a holdover from my ceremonial days), close everything up and get on with my day. It can be that simple. Elaborate does not necessarily equal good.

My general ritual outline: cleanse myself and my space; set up altar; cleanse some more; usually tend the ancestors before starting anything else; consecrate space (I use a fire chant, but this I *only* do for public rituals); transition into ritual (means will vary); pray and invoke; make offerings; meditate (sometimes make offerings after praying and meditating rather than before); when it feels right, give thanks; transition out; ground and center; do something to help cement the transition.

I'm not naming specific techniques because there are dozens and dozens of techniques and tools I could use. It'll vary depending on the ritual, the Deities involved, whether it's personal or public, etc. There's a fluidity here even when I have a set structure.

Suggestions:

Consider in your journal:

I. What do you think a ritual is?

II. Describe the best ritual you've ever experienced.

III. Describe the worst ritual you have ever experienced.

· ─ · · ─ · · ─ · · ─ · · ─ · · ─ · · ─ · · ─ · · ─ · · ─ · · ─ ·

To close this chapter, I want to share two articles that originally appeared as part of my "Heathen Heretic" column at witchesandpagans.com. The second is in response to the first. I've altered them slightly to fit the format of a book rather than a blog, but otherwise have made no changes. I do get a bit peppery – proper ritual is important to me.

Beltane Offerings

I recently posted a question on my Facebook, asking what recipes and dishes folks would suggest be made as offerings to Freya for Beltane. Cooking for the Gods, cooking up offerings is such a sacred rite in and of itself, and I can't help but wonder if our ancestors didn't have certain traditional foods or customary dishes (beyond roast pig) that were prepared for the various Powers. If they did, of course, we've lost that knowledge, but that doesn't mean that over time we won't regain it through the wisdom of our ancestors and inspiration of our Deities nor does it mean that we shouldn't give thought to what might please the various Gods and Goddesses the best right now. I very strongly believe that it's by engaging in devotion and working hard to strengthen the tradition and restore the lineage that such knowledge will be returned to us. Devotion is a powerful teacher in and of itself. So as I'm planning my House's Beltane celebration, I wanted to find out what foods other people customarily made for Freya at this time of year.

I had hoped (expected even) to get suggestions of specific dishes and some folks did come through to some extent. I came away from the conversation with a number of ideas that I wouldn't otherwise have had and which I'll share with you at the end. Unexpectedly, however, the conversation also highlighted yet another aspect of the devotional deficit so prevalent in contemporary Heathenry. I was really bowled over, though I suppose I shouldn't have been.

Suggestions ranged from having an eating contest ostensibly as part of the ritual, to getting drunk, to descriptions of ritual as "a party," with the tacit understanding that it was all about people socializing and not paying homage and veneration to the Gods.[1] There were repeated assumptions that the food being prepared would be consumed by the people, instead of being given as an offering and *left alone*. There was an over-focus on alcohol. I'm grateful to everyone who decided to offer suggestions, I really am. I think that people are doing their best to find their way often with a dearth of good role models. It is not my intention to attack any person who contributed to that discussion. I'm only going on the comments proffered and what I've seen directly in the community.

I was appalled. None of the suggestions given above have anything to do with a proper ritual. It took me awhile of pacing around my kitchen, smoking, and pondering to figure out what it was that was so 'off' to me. Firstly, any and all of the suggestions given are fine within the context of a *human-centered* social event. Have fun, behave boisterously, etc. I've no quarrel with any of that from the human side of things. I like a good party! For me, it's a question of time, place, and appropriate context. Is the ritual about me (or the people) or is it for and about the Gods (with the understanding that right relationship with the Gods benefits the

---

[1] The one exception to my hard line about ritual versus party is when the 'party' is focused in celebration of the God or Goddess in question, which in fact, is what my colleague, Mikki Fraser, was describing in the Facebook conversation I mention. While I agreed with his use of the term, it reminded me of other recent conversations where the idea of a 'party' as ritual was not so sanguine and it is to those latter aberrations that I speak here.

people)? That is the crucial question. As I was taught, rituals ought to be about encountering the sacred, about moving into space set aside from one's everyday life where one can engage with, honor, pay homage to, and celebrate the Gods – in the case of group rituals, as a community. I've said it before and I'll say it again: ritual should be focused on the Holy Powers (or in some cases the ancestors).

Now there are plenty of ceremonies that focus on the interstices between human and divine interaction, and even some – like coming of age rites – that make the transformation of the person involved their focus. Rituals like this have a good and necessary place. There are numerous ceremonies that salt the transitional times of a person's life with the sacred, like weddings and baby blessings. These, however, are not the type of rites of which I'm discussing here; I'm specifically focusing on devotional rituals to the various Powers.

I used to believe that people had an innate sense of reverence for the sacred...at least until I became Heathen. I've since come to rethink that. Whatever innate sense there might be in us is rapidly destroyed by the shallow, spiritually dead, disconnected culture in which we live and if that doesn't do the trick, it seems like modern Heathenry is hell bent on finishing the job. When I hear comments like, "I guess I tend to blur the lines between ritual and a party so we all have a good time," it's enough to make me weep. Some lines ought not to be blurred and if honoring the Gods isn't a joy, if it isn't a "good time," then I have to ask why one is even in the religion.

I'm sure by this time I must sound like a completely pompous prat. I can live with that if that's what it takes for me to openly address this issue. It seems more and more – and I am not the only one to have noticed this – that far too many Heathens (and this may hold true for Pagans too, but here I'm focusing on Heathenry) go out of their way to make their rituals as secular as possible. Oh, the Gods are a nice *idea* I suppose, but the reality of actual ongoing veneration and right relationship something quite different, and something most Heathens would, I suspect, rather avoid. All too often the religious side of Heathen rituals seems little more than play acting, something to be gotten through as quickly as possible (and with as little unnecessary emotion as possible, please) so folks can get down to what's really important: socializing. I do hope you read my sarcasm into this last statement, because it was there.

I think Heathenry as a whole is embarrassed by its Gods, by the actual realities of devotion so there is a concerted attempt to root it out of the religion, as if by distancing themselves from belief and active veneration, from anything approaching piety, the rest of the world – the monotheistic influenced, post modern world – might take them seriously. Devotion after all is so déclassé and having so many Gods is messy. Hear the sarcasm again?

My colleague Sarduriur Freydis Sverresdatter put it thusly:

What is the point of having special terms and functions and Gods – religion – if all one does is try to bludgeon the religiosity out of it all?

From where I'm standing, it looks as though they enjoy having an idea of the Gods around, but only as an idea. I think part of their apparent reluctance stems from their desire to appear 'enlightened' in the eyes of the rest of society.

They're not attempting to reconstruct a religious platform from which to build and grow and change healthily. No. They're attempting to reconstruct the culture. Which is sick. Knowing what I know of Medieval societies from my academic discipline…no. Just no. They were/are not desirable societies in which to live, especially if you were/are female. Scandinavian societies didn't always suck as much as, say, Burgundian or Frankish society, but they were almost as bad. What functions Gods and Goddesses played religiously, and how deities treated one another mythically, was/is not a reflection of the law, and how everyday people were treated. It was fucking hell. And these hardcore Recons want to bring these antiquated societal models back: treat women like chattel, hurl crude wood spears at each other to settle disputes, dress in (historically inaccurate) Medieval clothing, and get drunk off their asses *kind of* for the sake of communing with the Gods, but not really.

And they think that by distancing themselves from active belief and worship of Gods, from popular piety, the rest of the world will take them seriously.[2]

Which brings me right back to my initial question: is ritual a thinly veiled social hour or is it about the Gods? Time and time again in Heathen rituals, I've seen it be a real fight to get the average person to give generously to their Gods and ancestors. I'm sorry, a couple of drops of alcohol simply doesn't cut it. Unless that's really all one can afford to give, it seems so incredibly paltry in light of all the many blessings the Gods and ancestors have given and continue to give to us; and I've seen some people complain about giving that! It's as though somewhere along the way the community decided stinginess must be one of the nine noble virtues.[3]

Of course, to be fair, this is not representative of every single Heathen in the United States. There are many Heathens who are very devoted to their Gods, Goddesses, and ancestors and who do their best to maintain right relationship with Them. What I'm talking about, however, represents an attitude that is, nevertheless, endemic to the community as a whole. To me, this is a tremensdously sad state of affairs. I believe that we should go to the Gods

---

[2] This is quoted, with permission, from an online conversation with Sarduriur Freydis Sverresdatter. It should be noted that her academic discipline is Medieval history.

[3] This is part and parcel of the doggedly Protestant mentality that permeates so much of contemporary American Heathenry. Inevitably, people will reference the *Runatal* section of the *Havamal*, one of the lays of the *Poetic Edda* and the line "tis better not to give than to give too much..." This line of course refers specifically to negotiating with rune spirits. It does not in fact refer to offerings to the Gods or dead, but it provides a convenient excuse to the lore thumper to avoid stepping into a generous, reciprocal relationship of gift giving with the Powers.

with joy, with our hands and hearts full of offerings and our lips full of praise. We simply cannot give Them too much. The same holds true for our ancestors.

Part of this attitude both of ingrained penury and of aversion to the sacred comes from the exclusion – conscious and unconscious – of the sacred from our holy rites. Symbel and blót as they've come down to us through the surviving lore in no way represent the best of Heathen ritual praxis.[4] They have little to do with the Gods (though I have seen powerful blóts that were fully focused on the Gods, at the same time, in many instances, they stifled individual expression of devotion. It seems we've yet to find anything approximating a happy medium). Instead, the average Heathen ritual, drawn from these frameworks, focuses almost exclusively on people. The Gods are little more than an afterthought. I've attended Heathen rituals where a horn of mead was passed around and people were encouraged to hail their Gods. Few managed more than a "Hail, Thor." If one cannot take the time and care to craft a few simple words of devotion again I ask: why bother? Giving the least seems too much for many of us.

I love my religion. I love the Gods and Goddesses. I love my ancestors. It hurts seeing how tangled and devotionally neglectful Heathenry currently is. It could be so much more and I believe it should be. Devotionally clumsy would be okay – we all are clumsy in our devotions at times. But that's not what I see. I see hostility and aversion.

I think as a society, and as a community we're all self-centered enough. When entering ritual space, our focus must of necessity

---

[4] Given that the few accounts we have were largely recorded by Christians after conversion, Christians who had little interest in preserving the minutiae of polytheistic devotional practice, it's unlikely that they're entirely accurate. Nor were the surviving historical and literary texts we so facilely refer to as 'the lore' ever intended to be utilized as religious resources. Their purpose was never the preservation of Heathen practice. We must therefore be very careful when reading these texts for insight, not to take them as literal and thoroughly accurate accounts. In many cases (such as *Hakon the Good's Saga*, from which we get an account of symbel) we're dealing with fiction.

change from ourselves to the Powers. If that doesn't happen, regardless of the external structure, it's not a ritual. Or rather it's a very poorly run one. So how *do* I think a ritual ought to run? Well, 'ritual' can encompass many different elements. It should ideally be a flexible practice, a process whereby one engages with the sacred in a meaningful, committed way. It can be simple or elaborate. The important thing is that one's focus shifts to experiencing and honoring the sacred. That being said, I'll describe a bit of how I and those in my House might go about it.

For me, planning and facilitating a ritual takes at least a week's preparation. Usually, I start planning out all the particulars a couple of weeks ahead of time. A few days before the rite, I'll decide on what food and drink offerings are going to be made. I want to be clear, this is food for the Deity or Deities in question, or the ancestors. It is not something that the people gathered will touch. You don't give food and then take it back and really, we all get to indulge our appetites quite enough. A ritual is not party time. (We always have a potluck after our rituals and folks hang out and, if they wish, party then, so the human part of the equation does not go without).

A couple of weeks before the ritual, I'll start doing extra devotions to whatever Deity or Deities I intend to honor in the ritual. This may include praying to Them before I do the grocery shopping and as I'm preparing the food (which I will likely do the day before the rite), and letting Them know what I'm doing and why. The cooking is a ritual in and of itself for me. Sometimes I will do divination to figure out exactly what is desired as an offering. I'll email all the members of the House the pertinent information about the rite, including a list of appropriate offerings. The night before, I go over my own checklist to make sure I haven't forgotten anything.

The morning of the ritual, I will set up the altar which may include moving pieces from my personal shrines to the main, House altar. I'll attend to all the ritual cleansing of space and then, about a half hour before the ritual starts, I'll put out all of the food and drink offerings, grouping them as prettily as possible on the altar.

As people arrive, they know from experience to put their own offerings out. They'll be formally offered during the ritual.

People mill around chatting and catching up before ritual but once the ritual actually starts, everyone's focus is on honoring the ancestors and Holy Powers. That's the important part of a ritual, at least I think so: respect and mindfulness. We don't script our rituals. We don't have to. I have an outline of what needs to happen in my head, and we allow the rest of it all to flow. I make sure that everyone knows what to expect and what is and is not appropriate before the ritual ever begins. Once it does so, the Powers are invoked, many prayers made, there may be music, full prostration, offerings formally given, a horn passed around – the actual internal elements of each ritual may vary but the common thread uniting them all is respect.

Our rituals are not solemn either. We have a hell of a good time. Devotion is, at its heart, a celebration after all. But for the time the ritual proceeds, the focus is not on us. After the rite is concluded, folks eat, drink, and make merry all they want. There is, I think, a palpable sense of moving into the sacred, experiencing that engagement with the holy, and then transitioning back into 'regular' headspace and place again. At some point, some of us will dispose of the offerings in whatever way divination has deemed appropriate (sometimes that occurs later, or even the next day).

While this may seem like a lot, in reality it's all part of the ritual process. I don't think ritual needs to be a daunting process either. What I do on a day-to-day basis is very simple. The description above is that of a major House ritual, not what I do by myself to maintain my devotions. Ritual doesn't have to be fancy, in fact, some of the most powerful ones that I've experienced have been simple and to the point. What I believe and what I teach is absolutely required, is that mindfulness, that art, practice, and discipline of keeping one's mind centered not on the delights of socializing with one's neighbor, but, from the time the ritual proceeds, on the Gods. It's really not that difficult. One just has to want to do it, to see value in it, and then, to commit. My colleague Mikki Fraser put it best: "The god/dess needs to stay the focus of the ritual, otherwise it's too easy to make the whole thing a game or an ego trip."[5]

In the end, do whatever it is you do to honor the Powers, just do it with focus and mindful devotion *on* those Powers. From that, everything else will ultimately flow: from the blessings the Gods bestow to the reclamation of our traditional ways.

What did I finally come up with, by the way, as a result of the initial question? What foods will I be making for Freya? I did promise to tell you. I received many, many great suggestions as a result of the aforementioned conversation and after careful consideration, I decided to give Her the following:

* a plate of appetizers: oysters, smoked fish, large Spanish olives, and caviar
* several bars of various types of high quality chocolate
* strawberries: chocolate covered Godiva strawberries and also a bowl of regular strawberries coated in honey
* bananas with marshmallows and chocolate syrup
* Godiva chocolate liquor
* Goldschlager or champagne
* roasted pork loin with baked apples
* fresh asparagus
* potatoes au gratin
* honey
* crème brûlée
* chicken with honey-beer sauce
* baby back ribs
* cake
* good milk-stout
* a baked fish dish

My friend Elizabeth V. suggested offering several bags of cat litter and then donating them to an animal shelter, pointing out that

---

[5] This is quoted, with permission, from a private conversation Mikki and I had on Facebook.

she's found Freya to have a very protective interest in felines. Given
that there's a cat shelter in my town always in need of funds, I
might do that as well. Then of course, there are whatever offerings
House members bring. I'm sure there will be amber, perfume,
jewelry, and a plethora of other items as well for Her. At the end of
the ritual, the objects offered will either be burned, buried, or given
to the river behind my house and the food will be taken to the
woods behind my house and poured or placed out.

More on Ritual Praxis

So my recent "Heathen Heretic" article and its reception led me
to a certain epiphany with regard to the way so many of us
approach ritual. Let me begin by saying that I'm always surprised
when people purposely, or so it often seems, miss the point of my
articles. A colleague recently pointed out that much of my writing
provokes people past their comfort zones and that too rather
surprised me: that people would draw lines against experience and
narrow their worlds down to such small, grey places. Oh well. We
do, and everything in our world encourages us to do this, so I guess
I shouldn't be surprised. Still, there is nothing in my practice that
should be radical to someone engaged in deep devotion with their
Gods. Nothing.

So when my call for respect and piety as part of the ritual
process raised such a din, I was rather surprised. Then I realized,
that as with so much else, it all comes down to what one determines
is the purpose of ritual. It's more than just determining to place the
Gods at the center of the experience, though that is a huge part of
it, rather it's understanding why we are doing any of this ritual
'stuff' in the first place. What's the point? Whom does it benefit?
Obviously I believe it's at least desirable, if not crucial, or I wouldn't
be doing it. I think we forget that there are two sides of the
equation in any ritual process: the human side and the Other (Gods,
ancestors). The ritual itself is a conversation, ideally a dance
between those two factions. It's a means of communication and
experience. I suspect that's what makes rituals that are focused on
the Gods so threatening to some: they put something greater than

85

we above the sum total of our limited human experience. They connect us with that Other.

In response to my initial article, one woman told me privately that I had to remember that not everyone has the level of devotion she and I exhibit, that the majority of attendees to any ritual were laity. I found that comment very enlightening. Of course, I also found the reality of ritual demographics completely irrelevant to the ritual process itself. I don't think ritual is there to entertain or amuse the people. I think ritual is something that enables us to be in right relationship and communication with the Holy. It's a means, a technology whereby people are able to do that. A well-enacted ritual nourishes us as much as it hopefully pleases and nourishes the Gods. If we're clergy and the majority of people attending our rites are laity then we have an even deeper obligation to be good role models, to resist watering down our rites to cater to the inexperience and in many respects indolence of those attending. It's not about *us* and it shouldn't be stripped of its power in order to accommodate us. Gods know our people need good role models most especially in the areas of devotion and liturgical practice!

That is a huge part of the problem right there: by and large our communities lack good role models in the realm of ritual praxis; then, add that to the overwhelming majority of converts (in Heathenry at least) from Protestant denominations with their emphasis on gnosis through textual study rather than actual experience and ritual praxis, throw in a mix of people coming from New Age practices which in my opinion are really little more than shallow feel good pabulum or thinly veiled monotheism, and you've a recipe for....really boring rituals, rituals that forget the Other part of the devotional equation, rituals where the primacy goes to the people and their comfort, rituals that might be disrespectful and even impious.

As I said in my first article, there are ceremonies that attend to the needs of the people (weddings for instance, or house blessings, or coming of age ceremonies) but devotional rites are not that type of ceremony. For many other Heathens and Pagans I encounter, ritual is apparently only about tending to the needs of the people, with the Gods coming in (at least as seems to me) a far second. In some cases, I've come to suspect that the rituals are structured to keep the Gods as far away as possible, to dispense with sacred obligations in as unsecured and terse a means as possible, and to prevent actual experience and certainly to eschew ecstasy. For those of you reading this, if this is the only kind of ritual experience that you have ever known, I'm sorry. I feel sorry for you and I very much wish that your experiences had been different.

I was talking about this with friend of mine from school, a seminarian (and brilliant Latinist, I might add) and he quipped that with all the infighting centering around this issue and in response to my article, we all sounded like a bunch of Catholic versus Protestant liturgists in the debate on ritual, and in many respects he's right. This is something that Christianity has wrestled with at least since the 1960's and probably beyond. In fact I'd take it right back to the Protestant Reformation and the iconoclasms that followed. The tension between traditional Deity-centered ritual and feel good, accessible people-centered ritual mirrors the tensions between traditional and modern modes of worship.

What we're really dealing with is the commoditization of spirituality and the moment we start looking at spiritual engagement in that light, it loses any measure of integrity or power. My Latinist friend put it succinctly: "And remember this: We are all a bunch of corporatist, capitalist, decadent, self-absorbed whores, aka consumers. We consume. One of the products we consume is religion."

I would like to think my friend is just being overly cynical but it does make me wonder. The above mentioned liturgical divide mirrors one that I see again and again cropping up in Heathenry: is what we do for the people or for the Gods? Y'all know where I stand on that one. Anything less than a Deity-centered practice for me is spiritual masturbation. I was very, very lucky to have extremely good ritual training, both within the Fellowship of Isis and academically with ritual studies classes. Add on a seminary background, and twenty years running rituals and to my shock, I find I'm comfortable letting that process flow. (There was a time, when I was just starting out, where leading a ritual scared me!) I know that my job when I lead a ritual is to prepare properly, to hold the space, to guide people into a space and a head and heart place where they have the potential to engage with the Powers, and when that is over, guide them back to Midgard space again. My job is to hold the doorway open through which the human part and the Other part may have a conversation. My job is to ensure that the energy flows and focus stays on the Gods.

Now a couple of those commenting on my last article said that Heathens are devotionally aware, they just show it differently than I. If that is true than I think that maybe we're working off two very different ideas of what it means to be devotionally aware. I have found that once you've been in a ritual grounded in absolute respect and piety, where everyone's absolute focus to the best of their abilities is on joyously honoring the Gods, you know the difference and you know what you're missing. You know when devotion is present and when it's not. Piety and respect should not be classed as 'mysticism.' There's nothing 'mystical' about it, save that it's all too often as rare as a goddamned unicorn in our communities. Devotion isn't mysticism either. These things might take you into mystic straits as it were, but they are not in and of themselves mysticism. Nor should Heathen rites be the polytheistic equivalent of Protestant Sunday mass where you go, give up a brief amount of time where someone else does all the work, and then hurry off to potluck and coffee hour feeling good about yourselves. We can do better than that, for ourselves and for our Gods.

This isn't a game. The Gods are real and there are right and wrong ways to go about honoring Them. The right way isn't about any specific technique or tool, or garb or ideology, it's about respect, pure and simple. The Gods are capable of telling us what They want. They do it all the time. Proper ritual is a container within which we are able to safely – as much as anything sacred can be safe, which is often not so much – engage. This reality clashes up against Western hubris, which for generations and generations has taught us that we're the apex predators of the world, we're the center of the universe, the dominant intelligence, the *raison d'être*

that the sun shines. There's very little in our culture that encourages us to go beyond ourselves. We fight baggage we're often not even aware we're carrying but it's a fight in which the Gods and ancestors can help. The alternative is a ritual praxis and a religion that is all about reinforcing people's narrow comfort zones, reinforcing their arrogance, their hubris, allowing them to mill about playing at being sacred – with good hearts, mind you, I don't fault that, but play is still play – and excluding direct engagement with the Gods. The alternative is a religion that has very little to do with the sacred. Those of us involved in restoring tradition and building lineage need to ask ourselves if that's the road down which we wish to walk. For me and mine the answer is a most definite no.

Chapter 8:
Devotion in the World

This chapter is a bit more abstract than anything else that we've been talking about so far. I've noticed over the years that there's a certain unconscious preconception that in order to be devotional (which many people equate, however misguidedly with 'holy'), one must completely divorce oneself from the regular, quotidian world. Much of this comes from the influence of Christianity on our culture. Thus you may be familiar with the Christian idea of "in the world but not of it." While the ascetic's path is a valid one, and a very powerful and valuable calling for some people (likewise monasticism), it is not the only way to live a devotional life. There's a quote by the Sufi poet/mystic Rumi that I absolutely adore "there are thousands of ways to kneel and kiss the ground." He's right too. As polytheists we can absolutely live a full and vital life intimately connected to the richness of the world around us and at the same time live deeply devoted lives. There's no antagonism between the two there.

Now there are times where we might feel more strongly pulled to focus inward, on the interiority of practice that is so crucial for clean devotional work. As with so many other aspects of living and being there may be a subtle ebb and flow to what we're pushed to do devotionally. That's perfectly okay. I tend to look at it like a muscle: sometimes we expand and are focused more in the world, sometimes we contract and must nourish and nurture our interiority of practice and these two opposites complement and reinforce each other, making for clean, healthy movement forward. It's expansion and contraction and both are necessary. So, do not worry that you cannot be devotionally minded if you also have a family, a job, and other 'mundane' cares.

I think that the important thing is keeping the gods central to one's life. Devotion to Them should be the axis around which everything else revolves. I was recently having a conversation with someone who kept insisting that I tell him something about myself unrelated to my Gods. Neither I nor my partner could do it. I finally had to lay it out for him: there is nothing in my life unrelated to my polytheism. How I live my life is a direct result of the devotion I have for my Gods and ancestors. It informs every single aspect of 'me.' Everything I do, from studying Latin to painting and glassblowing, to the way I engage with friends is deeply informed in some way, shape, or form by my devotional connections and all of this has made me a better and more engaged human being. That is the way I believe that we are meant to be in the world. Keeping the Gods first doesn't mean that you withdraw from life, rather it informs every aspect of the way you engage with living. One of the many misconceptions that often arise is that keeping the Gods central to one's life means not only eschewing human engagement but devaluing it as well when nothing could be further from the truth. In reality, if you're doing this devotional thing right, it enhances everything. It changes the way that we engage because devotional awareness demands action. It demands that we wake up to our impact on the world around us and act accordingly because our Gods are not separate from the world, They are deeply entwined with it and interested in it.

So how does all this play out? Well, I have no idea, and that's largely because the result of this may be different for each and every one of us. The more deeply one engages with devotional work, the more one runs the risk of becoming aware of all the imbalances and damage in the world around us and that often carries with it a growing obligation to action. We are windows for our Gods in the world – not only a means by which They can experience us experiencing life, but a means by which we can carry Their medicine to all the broken places in our world. There is nothing insignificant about that.

Engagement with all those broken places in our world (and engagement with the beautiful, the inspiring, the loving) can be powerful acts of devotional offering. This runs the gamut from large to small, from responding to an incredibly annoying co-worker with compassion as a conscious act of offering to the Gods, to volunteering once a week at a soup kitchen, to fundraising for a cause to which you are committed, to cleaning up public parks, to tithing part of your income to a charity you support, to making art, caring for graves in a local cemetery, learning a language for your ancestors, raising your children in your faith – it really depends on the Deity. Think about the Deity and the areas of Their dominion and find things that are appropriate within that. It's an important step when we can allow the devotional consciousness that we've cultivated to change the way we live, and that change happens first in our headspace, in the way we look at things, in the awareness we bring to any situation. I have found over the years that this work *demands* that we work toward change in the world. How that happens though is very individualistic. Anything and everything can be done with devotional consciousness. Some things can be done as conscious offerings.

When I trained clergy over the years, one of the more controversial things (at least to my trainees) that I would require was four hours of volunteer work a month. This comes down to one hour a week or one half day a month and each student could choose what he or she did. It's not excessive. It always shocked me how resistant many of my trainees were to this. It offended several of them that they were expected to do something that involved shifting their focus off themselves and onto the world around them. (One of the reasons I did this was precisely for that reason: clergy cannot afford to separate themselves from the goings-on of the world, particularly those areas broken and fractured and in need of healing and nor is priestcraft an excuse to avoid active engagement in the world. The same holds true for devotional work.)

Some people will be called more to this type of active offering than others. For some people, activism and volunteer work is a deeply powerful means of connecting to and serving the Gods. That is one extreme. At the other end of the spectrum is the person who simply allows his or her devotional work to inform how he or she looks at and interacts with the world and those he or she encounters in it. In either case it's important not to think that doing something in the world is a substitute for worship. This is where I see the biggest chance of error: volunteer work, activism, charity...all of this is good and may be a valuable offering but it does not exempt one from the obligation of veneration. We don't get a pass because we're being nice. So there's a balance that has to happen here, and always the key is bringing one's awareness, focus, and attention back to the Gods and the Gods back to the center of one's life.

Suggestions:

Think about some ways that either individually or as a household you can allow your devotion to propel you into active engagement with the world. What can you do in this capacity as an offering? What do you already do?

Chapter 9:
Spiritual Trauma

One of the most difficult things to discuss about the devotional process is spiritual trauma. Part of living a deeply engaged spirituality often entails initiation, sometimes into various levels of a tradition, sometimes spurred by the Gods Themselves. There is danger here and I think this is something that so few people really want to talk about: initiatory experiences, even when they are well planned and formal, can shatter a person. This is par for the course. I know that those who are familiar with my writings on Northern Tradition shamanism and Raven Kaldera's writings know that we've talked about the trauma of becoming a shaman, how there is a psychic and sometimes physical death. That's *not* what I'm talking about here. I'm talking about what some spiritually-oriented psychologists term "spiritual emergency."

Think about it: devotional work entails a tremendous amount of vulnerability. Stepping into the presence of the Holy, even pre-paring yourself to do so, takes tremendous courage. Those experiences, (or an initiatory experience, or both) can shatter the paradigm with which you have been so comfortably ensconced for much of your life. In fact, they *need* to do that. They force us not only to see the world differently, and our place in it, but to see ourselves differently as well.

I have witnessed this type of experience (specifically formal initiation) bring up all the wounded, fractured places of the initiate. This was good and necessary – you don't build a house on a broken foundation right? The initiate had the community support and was at a place where theoretically she could choose to heal. This all sounds good....difficult but good, and it was, except that the woman in question chose not to deal with any of it. She chose to reinforce old, unhealthy relationship patterns, to self-medicate (!) instead of doing the internal work of learning to cope. She chose to be overwhelmed – and make no mistake, it was a choice – rather than do the work that was now her portion by virtue of initiation. Spiritual work breaks us open and sometimes there's a period of crazy that we go through before adjusting to that. Sometimes, some folks choose not to adjust. Either way, it leaves us forever changed. This is where building up a really solid foundation from the very beginning is so terribly, terrifyingly crucial.

I am purposely emphasizing the choice here. I would say that it is quite often the case – to be fair, not always; those who weren't properly prepared, who have little support, etc., may be washed away faster than they can hope to gain purchase – but in most cases, whether or not one breaks is a personal choice. Whether or not one makes it through is a choice, just like devotion and faith is an ongoing everyday choice. *This* is where a dedicated, pious community, who understood and moreover *valued* spirituality and devotional connections, would be invaluable. This is where teachers and elders and a community that understood and honored their wisdom and importance to the tradition would be invaluable. This is where not pathologizing the spiritual process or medicating it away would be abso-fucking-lutely invaluable. We have, of course, none of those things.

Also, not to be discounted is the fact that there is a specific psychological process inherent in conversion and if it's done well, it involves a radical shift in paradigm. None of this is easy particularly when there is so little adequate community support. One book that I highly recommend is *Spiritual Emergency* by Stanislav and Christina Grof. It's a classic in the field. What I tell people is this: understand that this path is fraught with potential trauma. The reasons behind that are manifold: we're being honed as human beings by our Gods (and probably ancestors); we're having our emotional wounds brought up so that we can heal them rather than push them down; we're having our paradigms realigned; we're growing. Understand that this process is difficult, sometimes incredibly painful but understand too that you're not going through it alone. Your Gods and ancestors are there for you to call upon. If you're lucky you have elders, teachers, a support network, but if not, trust your Gods to see you through. Trust and hold to that devotional relationship like a lifeline. Do not give up. Many, many devotionally aware people have treaded this road before you. Christianity even has a ton of literature on this, starting with St. John of the Cross's *Dark Night of the Soul*. It's a time when we're forced to face our wounds, our fears, and most of all our doubts and are charged with finding the fortitude to heal and overcome them because devotional work is *hard*. The main difference between ongoing pathology and a spiritual crisis or emergency is that the latter is ultimately very, very beneficial. It results and resolves in a stronger, more connected, healthier, more whole human being. In many respects the spiritual crisis is an inevitable threshold that we all at some point must choose to cross.

In many traditions (particularly the African Traditional Religions), one is encouraged to see a skilled diviner every three months. This is certainly what I was taught and is in part to help navigate the challenges of spiritual transformation. This has a couple of benefits: the client has the direct engagement with an elder; that elder – a diviner – can prepare the client for upcoming spiritual challenges, can be a support through them providing guidance from the perspective of one who has hopefully been through those dark places, and can also suggest offerings and prayers that may help navigate that terrain. The way, after all, can seem very bleak and dark when one is in the midst of such a spiritual descent. The other thing that I want to emphasize is that really, the only way out is through.

What a way to recommend devotional work, right? I will say this: I've been through those dark places several times and in each case I've come out stronger and closer to my Gods. That process rips away the brittle masks of our ego, it helps us cleanse ourselves of all those things that keep us from seeing clearly, that keep us mired in the masks and facades a very diseased world creates. This is a necessary and *good* process but oh, it is hard. All the steps that you take devotionally up to that point, though, from the very first fumbling, faltering ones, teach little by little the necessary tools to help see you through. By the time we hit one of these challenging times, we have deep within us – whether we realize it or not – the tools we need to make it through.

◆—— · · —— · · —— · · —— · · —— · · —— · · —— · · —— · · —— · · —— · · —— · ◆

Suggested Reading:

In the meantime, here is some suggested reading. I don't agree with all of it, but it'll help provide some background:

http://spiritualemergency.blogspot.com/2006/01/defining-spiritual-emergency.html

http://www.stanislavgrof.com/pdf/viggiano.and.krippner.pdf

http://www.ccel.org/browse/bookInfo?id=john_cross/dark_night

Some Closing Thoughts

To close Part One of this book, I want to offer a few final suggestions for those just beginning their devotional journey. The best thing that I can suggest with regard to devotional practice is to do it. Be consistent, especially in facing the resistance and often difficult emotions that can arise. Be brave and be consistent.

As an aside, it helps to read devotional literature to some degree, even if it's not polytheist; but I've also found that one must be careful to filter out some of the more egregiously monotheistic overtones. Being triggered by something is not bad, but not examining and sorting through the reasons behind the triggering can be. I often struggle with this myself, because I find Catholic devotional literature, particularly hagiographies of the saints, very helpful – but sooner or later one runs up against the fixation on Jesus or the monotheism and it can be deeply disturbing. I consciously deal with those emotions and try to take what is useful from the text. If I can't do that, I find another text. I don't torture myself.

Finding a community, even if it is dispersed online, of like-minded people with whom you can discuss devotion and who can encourage you, and vice versa, is also helpful. I am deeply suspicious, though, of anything or anyone that attempts to lighten or lessen my devotional attentions so be on your guard. You will find this in abundance by people who are triggered by it, resentful of it, jealous, or any one of a dozen other emotions. As the saying goes, keep your eye on the prize – in this case, keep focused on the Gods and ancestors and do not let community shit pull your focus away. This is sometimes, even for me, easier said than done!

Also, don't get overly invested in external side effects of your devotional work. You don't need bling (though I understand the desire to give pretty things to the Gods, and share it) and you

98

should be wary of expecting that the Gods will want to step in and govern the day-to-day minutiae of your life. If that's happening, I tend to think of it as wish fulfillment rather than actual devotional engagement (though there are exceptions). I tell people: don't go seeking taboos. If you're meant to have them, they will come. Moreover, every time you invite a God in to micro-manage your affairs, a debt is being incurred and you may find them coming sooner than you expected or truly desired. It is normal and even good to want to do things to remind ourselves of the daily devotional practice, of our relationship with our Gods, of the Gods Themselves, but it's important to really recognize what is coming from the Gods and your engagement, and what is coming from the deep hungers in your mind and heart and soul. Do what you need to do to further your devotional awareness but don't invest it with any excessive import. It's way too easy to get caught up in minutiae. There's nothing wrong with keeping it simple; it allows for more laser-like focus.

What *You* Can Do

Sometimes people ask me, "How can I do what you do?" On occasion, this question is asked by someone who is a new spirit-worker, part of the younger, up-and-coming generation of shamans, mystics, spiritworkers, godspouses, etc.; more often, however, it's asked by a nice 'normal' person, leading a nice 'normal' life, wanting to know what he or she can do to become more engaged, to do what they perceive as 'important' work for their Gods and ancestors.[1]

This question comes from a good and well-meaning place. I think it's a very good thing, crucial even, to want to become more involved, to want to better serve the Gods and spirits. At the same time, this question bothers me on a number of levels.

---

[1] For the record, I vehemently dislike the word 'normal.' I don't think 'normal' exists. I think there is what is normal for Galina, what is normal for Susan, what is normal for David, etc. There is no one 'normal' just damaging, limiting boxes we try to squeeze ourselves into – to our own detriment.

Firstly, you can't do what I do. You're not Galina. You can't do Galina's work. You can only do *your* work. It may be similar but it may be something totally different, something that I couldn't do in a million years. It's important that you do your work not mine and not anyone else's. The Gods have a Galina. They don't need another one. They need a Jack and a Joan and a John and a Jill doing their individual work. It's *all* important. I think one of the most damaging things for one's spiritual life is trying to fit yourself into someone else's box. You have to do your own work, walk your own path, even if it bears no resemblance to mine, *most especially* if it bears no resemblance to mine. We can support each other in this but we can't do each other's work.[2]

I fight with exactly this type of spiritual envy sometimes. I have friends who are amazing painters, photographers, musicians, artists of one sort or another and I dabble and I sometimes catch myself thinking wistfully on their talent and wishing with an ache and a longing that I could do what they do. I can't, no matter how much I wish it, and were I to fixate on it, were I to try to force myself into a mold for which I am unsuited and uncalled, the work that *is* mine to do would not get done. My spiritual life would wither. I'd be betraying my wyrd and my Gods.

I've learned over the years when I feel this way to consciously say to myself: "Well, I can't do that, but they can and wow, I can sure appreciate it and I can let them know what joy their work brings me. I can even share it with others." Appreciating beauty is important too. Our world needs all the beauty it can get. It has the power to heal, to transform, to inspire.

Secondly, there's something about this question that seems to devalue the life one is living. Just because one isn't a spiritworker doesn't mean that one's life and work and spirituality lack value. Do I think that shamans and spiritworkers are crucial to their communities? Absolutely, especially now with how out of balance

---

[2] This is one of the terrifying responsibilities of teaching. One can guide and encourage but to force someone into a mold unsuited to them is a grave wrong, a spiritual crime even.

our world has gotten. Part of our job is to restore right relationship and to navigate the worlds of the spirits. But that doesn't mean that I think a farmer or a shopkeeper or an auto mechanic or a computer programmer is any less important. It's not an either/or. It's *all* important. Each of us has a place and a function that's valuable. I would like us to move away from placing such arbitrary value judgments on our jobs. (If you ask me, the most important job in the world is sanitation engineer….think about it, folks. seriously. Think about it.)

That my writing focuses on the work of a shaman and spiritworker is a matter of this being my calling. If I were a blacksmith, I'd be writing about that (or not writing probably, but turning out some fabulous metalwork). One doesn't have to be a shaman to be doing useful work. If the Gods wanted everyone to be a shaman, They could make that happen. Obviously, They prefer a little diversification of calling.

The question remains: if one is living the life and doing the work that one is meant to be doing, (let's presuppose that for the sake of this question), honoring one's ancestors in whatever way works within one's personal practice, but one is not a shaman, mystic, or spiritworker, what can one do to help with the Work? To do more? To become more engaged?

What I think people are really asking in many cases when this question arises is, "What can I do that's important?" We all want to feel valued and important, after all, and I have found that many, many people want to be part of what a shaman or spiritworker does, because they feel it brings them closer to the Gods. I get that. They want to be part of something. Well, you are already 'part of something' but there *is* a very powerful answer to this question; there is something that everyone can be doing, something that was and is done in almost every indigenous culture that's still rooted in its ancestral ways the world over: pray.

For those wanting to be part of the work that a shaman or spiritworker does, for those wanting to become more engaged, to touch the sacred a little more directly, for those wanting to do something absolutely and utterly crucial with respect to engaging with the Gods and spirits then do this: pray for your spiritworkers. Pray for your shamans. Pray for your mystics. Pray for those actively engaging with the Gods and spirits. Pray for anyone undergoing a 'dark night of the soul' be they shaman, spiritworker, or regular Joe. Pray consistently. Just pray. Pray for your technicians of the sacred.

And pray for all our ancestors: yours, mine, your friends', your enemies' ancestors, *all* our ancestors. Pray that they are strengthened. Pray that they have the strength and courage, wisdom and perseverance to step forward and partner with their living in this work (and that 'Work' is comprised of each and every one of us doing that which we were put here to do, be it spiritwork, raising a family, or being an accountant!). Pray that they lend us their strength and their protection.

I talk a lot about fighting the Filter, about the need for every single person to engage in this battle. Well, here's one of the most powerful tools at your disposal: prayer. It is in no way insignificant. Moreover, in functioning indigenous communities, it was the sacred work of the community to pray for their spiritworkers, just as it was the sacred work of the spiritworker to navigate the spirit worlds and interface with Gods and spirits for the community. This was a win-win situation. That prayer part of the equation is fundamental and crucial.[3]

So when you ask me, "How can I do what you do?" don't be surprised if I look you in the eye and say, "You can't." But you can

---

[3] My colleague Sarenth and I were discussing the corollary to this: that the community may ask their shamans, spiritworkers, priests and mystics to pray for them. Sarenth said, "I would also suggest they ask their spiritworkers and shamans to pray for them. I would have no issue keeping a list of people to pray for at my altar, for individual names, or even whole groups. I wouldn't mind praying for others' Dead, especially if they cannot keep an active shrine. I can see how that can be abused, but I also can see this as establishing gebo. We can, and should pray for one another. Enough of us are in rough spots that we all could use the prayers!" He's right and many of us have been doing this as a matter of course: praying regularly for those who ask but it wasn't until our conversation that I realized many may not know to ask.

pray and we need you to pray, we need that desperately. It is important work. It is absolutely necessary and it's work that each and every one of us can do.

"If you're breathing, you can be praying." – Setep

Part Two of this book offers a mini 'book of hours,' daily rituals that one can do to connect and reconnect devotionally. They are Heathen rituals, but each provides a very, very simple format that can easily be adapted by those of other polytheistic traditions. I encourage readers to adapt these basic rites. Write your own prayers, develop your own nightly meditations. This is the next step in figuring out what works and putting it all together in practice.

PART TWO

Daily Rites: Marking the Week with the Gods

In the realm of devotion, Heathens are fortunate in that we have some idea of how our ancestors' weekly sensibilities were ordered. The very names of the days of the week reflect etymological associations with certain Deities. So we have Monday associated with the moon and Mani, Tuesday with the God Tiw or Tyr, Wednesday with Woden, and Thursday with Thor. Friday has disputed associations with *either* Freya or Frigga (so I've chosen to include devotional rites to Them both here; that seemed better to me than excluding either Goddess) and Saturday is another conundrum. For some reason, the name that has come down to us is drawn from the Roman God Saturn. We've no idea to which of our Holy Powers this day was originally given. For that reason, I've chosen to give this day to Loki and nor am I the only Loki devotee to do so. Now Loki is a very controversial Deity within contemporary Heathenry. Because we don't know what Deity originally owned this day, and because not every contemporary Heathen may honor Loki, readers should feel free to adapt Saturday's rite to serve the needs of any Deity they choose to honor on this day. Sunday of course, belongs to the Sunna, the Sun Goddess. She is sometimes referred to as Sol.

In this section, you will find a very simple devotional rite for each day of the week. Each ritual honors the God or Goddess associated with that particular day and, in addition to the daily meditations given in the first section of this book, may be performed at the opening or close of the day as directed. Readers should feel free to adapt and alter these rites to suit their own needs, for what is presented here is only a very simple guide providing the basic structure of such rites. Additionally, these rituals are intended for the solitary practitioner, but may be adapted for family worship.

I encourage everyone to create their own rituals. This is an art form, a skill that can be learned. As with any other craft, it requires practice and there may be a learning curve. As a basic guide, it's important to keep in mind that when you craft a ritual, either for yourself or others, you are in some way drawing the attendees into a shared experience of the sacred. If you are doing ritual for yourself, then you are bringing yourself into a carefully crafted time and place wherein you can thoroughly focus on and engage with the Sacred. There's no real right or wrong way to do that save one: the rule of thumb, particularly when one is invoking or praying to one's Holy Power(s), is simple: respect. Every part of the ritual, every action, every prayer should in some way draw attention to the Deity being honored, or, barring that, to the purpose of the rite. For instance, don't stop in the middle of a ritual to discuss trivialities with a friend who is also present. Make sure your cell phone and home phones are turned off. Do what you can to, if not eliminate, at least minimize distractions.

While the structure and ingredients of a ritual are limited only by your own imagination and creative impulse, let every single element and action be guided by, if not devotion, then at the very least respect. This is the one hard and fast rule of ritual praxis. Beyond that, you're limited only by your creativity. Any tools that you choose to use or to omit – a pretty altar, music, incense, chanting – are only that: tools designed to help one better enter into the spiritual, emotional, and mental receptivity necessary for such spiritual engagement to occur.

This is not to say that mistakes won't happen. They will; but when they do, simply respectfully bring your own attention back to the purpose at hand, the reason behind the ritual, and continue on. Mistakes are not synonymous with lack of devotional respect or ritual protocol.

Rituals, as you will see from those given here, need not be fancy. You are simply making time and space in which to connect with the Holy Powers, and to honor Them in some structured way.

It is a way of bringing yourself back to the goal of ordering your life around your devotion. I hope that is something that everyone reading this can see as a worthy goal, even if the way to do that is not always easy to discern. The word 'ritual' itself comes from the Latin word *ritus*, which means, in part, 'a religious custom.' That is really what ritual ought to be: a custom of turning one's attention to the Gods. All the formal rites in the world are just one's expression of that praxis. How you choose to do your own rituals is entirely up to you. I offer those here as a very basic guide to get you started.

MONDAY: HONORING MANI, THE MOON GOD

For Heathens and Norse pagans, the moon Deity is male. He is a glorious, gentle, and deeply compelling God named Mani, the son of Time, nephew of Night, brother to the Sun and the Cosmos. He rides across the fabric of night, followed by the wolf Hati, who, it is said, either keeps Him on His course, or chases Him with the intent of devouring Him and bringing on Ragnarok. Only Mani knows the truth of the matter, and perhaps, the wolf. (January's moon is traditionally called 'wolf moon.' I wonder if there is a connection or if it is more that our ancestors found the wolves in the forests to howl with hunger in the frozen coldness of winter?)

What is attested to in the surviving sources, and in the experience of those devoted to Him, is how deeply Mani cares for humanity, especially children. Some say that it is for this reason that the wolf must follow Him, for otherwise He might easily be swayed off His course out of curiosity or caring for those humans who scurry about beneath the waxing and waning of the orb He bears.

Monday actually means 'moon-day' and I try to do a little something for Mani every Monday. Sometimes I forget – I'm human and I make mistakes. My mindfulness occasionally has its lapses. But I do my best to be as consistent as possible. Fortunately, even when I slip up, Monday will always come round again.

I like to give Him little things whenever I can. Usually, I make my offerings in the evening, because I like to do so when the moon is visible in the night sky. Sometimes though, He rides high and proud, winking at us from the lightening hues wrought by His sister's passage and for me, there's a special delight in that and then I will honor Him when I rise, making my offerings with the brightening day.

Offerings like this need not be enormous. I usually give Him a glass of either sambuca or Smirnoff's marshmallow-flavored vodka. He seems to like it. I spend a few moments in prayer and that's that until the next Monday. It's a stabilizing consistency to the crazy roller coaster of my life.

Some might find it strange that we honor a moon God and not a Goddess (our Sun Deity is a Sun Goddess as well – and Mani's sister – to complete the juxtaposition) but we are not unique in this: Japanese and Egyptian religions also have moon Gods and I suspect there are a few more as well. One wonders though if all the moon Gods are companions....

When my adopted mom was small she used to call the moon Luna Lunera and would watch as She (my mom of course as a small child thought the moon female) showered the earth with the blessings of her gentle light. She said her father would stand on a balcony of their home while she played in the garden and throw candies down and she thought they came from the moon. Maybe, in a way, they did.

I never thought about it one way or another until I encountered Mani and then I knew what it was to love the moon. He is beautiful and compelling in His ways. Even I am not immune, though it amuses many and probably Mani too should He ever catch wind of it.

Silently You watch
lovely in the hall of Night,
tempting all the worlds.

A Jotun told me
tales of You, that long ago
Your name was Longing.

It is a fable,
his heart's wish and yet my lips
whisper too: longing.

Evening Rite for Mani

Begin by setting up a small altar to Him. It need not be elaborate, but should include a candle and incense burner with incense. Moon images and anything else associated with the moon are quite appropriate. Many of us have found that Mani likes beaded necklaces, jangles, time pieces, even bits of clock and watch innards, abacuses, calendars, night blooming flowers, and music. Anything of this ilk, and anything else that one personally feels called to associate with or give to Him is appropriate to place on the altar. You should also have something to offer Him: a glass of alcohol, cookies, flowers….anything that you are moved to give. (If you are including your children in this ritual, have them help you prepare the altar).

Once you have created the altar, which is, in effect, an invocation in and of itself, sit quietly for a few moments centering yourself. This may easily be accomplished by the simple exercise described in Chapter 2 called the 'four-fold breath.' Repeat for five minutes continually.

Once you feel that you are adequately centered and focused, turn your attention to Mani. Envision the moon in the sky. Think about all that He must have seen as human civilization progressed, all that He must have witnessed. Imagine that you are reaching out to him with heart and hand and spirit. Imagine that, as you breathe, you are breathing in His silver, soothing light. You are filling yourself with the blessed touch of the moon. When you feel ready, light the candle with the words, "With this light, I kindle the light of the moon in my heart, in my mind, in my spirit."

Light a stick of incense and offer it with the words, "I offer this incense, that I might be blessed by Mani, son of time, keeper of the roads of night."

Invocation

Hail to Mani,
Hail to the God of the Moon.
Hail to the Sweet Light in the darkness,
and Sweet Darkness in the light.

Son of Time, be with me here tonight.
Turn Your gentle gaze in my direction.
Wash me in the sweet caress of Your light.

Allow me to thank You for Your blessings-
especially for the grace of my day.
I know each day is a gift.
Thank you for seeing me through
and thank you for watching over me each night.
By Your grace, may I never lose my awareness of Your blessings.

Ride swiftly across the darkness, Sweet God of the Moon.
May You always outpace the wolf who nips at Your heels.
I hail You Mani with gratitude.
I hail You with love.
I shall hail You always,
in adoration.
Hail best loved son of Mundilfari.

Offering

Set out any offerings that you wish to give to Him. This can be as simple as a single glass of alcohol, or a cookie.

Meditation

Spend a few moments in contemplation. As you sit in silence, imagine that with each breath you are drinking in the presence and blessings of the moon. With each inhalation you are inhaling Mani's soothing, healing light. Feel or imagine that this light flows through you cleansing away all stress and tension, and any miasma you may have picked up throughout your day.

Continue for as long as you like praying or meditating upon the blessings of the Moon.

Closing Prayer

Thank you, Mani, for holding me in Your light.
May my comings and goings on this day be pleasing to You.
Hail Mani, always.

The rite is now completed. You can either allow the candle to burn down, or save it for your next Mani ritual. I usually find it best to leave the altar out for awhile, but there is nothing amiss if you must, of necessity, deconstruct it right after the rite.

I think that this ritual is best done before bed, but this is a very personal matter. Some people are simply more alert in the morning. Being a night owl, I tend to prefer doing all my ritual work late in the day or early evening. Use your own judgment in this. Do this rite whenever you feel you can best connect to Mani.

Suggestions for Mani

(In each of the rituals for the days of the week, I provide a small section of similar suggestions. These suggestions have been drawn from my own experience with the God or Goddess in question, and discussions with many others who honor Him. They are suggestions and you should not feel limited by them. If you want to offer something not on this list, or feel a strong association, go with it).

Colors: blues, silvers, black, purple/lavender, pale white
Symbols: anything moon-shaped, hour glasses, old watches, clocks, and their component parts, knots, calendars, musical scores, flutes, beads, mirrors, mathematical equations, abacuses and other time keepers, astrolabes and other nautical equipment for plotting directions
Stones: moonstone, labradorite, selenite, quartz, and amethyst
Flowers: camellias, jasmine, night blooming flowers
Food and drink: sambuca, cookies (especially ones with

marshmallows or odd shapes; a nice way to incorporate children into the above ritual, is to have them make moon shaped cookies in honor of Him), angel food cake, peppermint flavored sweets

Other offerings: any volunteer work or donations that benefit abused children or the mentally ill

Contraindicated: harming or abusing children in any way; mocking the mentally ill

TUESDAY: HONORING TYR, GOD OF JUSTICE

I was born on a Tuesday and it's a day that belongs to the God Tyr. The Romans syncretized Him with Mars as a God of war. I understand that. For me, it makes sense not because He is our sword-God but because He is the God of the necessary action….not the honorable action, not the 'good' action, not justice and mercy in the way that Forseti (a God of magistrates and judges if ever I saw one) might be, but necessary action – and that is a thing that warriors know well. It is one of those shadowy realities that lie at the core of warrior medicine: an understanding of necessary versus good and a willingness to do the former. That is where Tyr stands. That is His warrior's wound. That is the source of His power.

Tuesday is His day: Tyr's Day. I don't have much of a relationship with Him beyond the most peripheral despite my work with the warrior dead. There are other Warrior Deities that came calling for me first. Still, I honor Him on His day with simple offerings.

Usually I give Him a glass of whiskey or whatever other strong spirits I have in my home. I will offer a brief prayer and then set it out on generic altar space (He does not have a shrine in my home – not for lack of respect but for the simple reason that I've never felt called to give Him one and with upwards of 50 shrines in my house, I only really put them up when I feel a push to do so) and I offer a small prayer. Duty done until the next Tuesday.

So hail the God of a warrior's justice,
the God of necessary things,

necessary choices
that defy the honor
found therein.
He did what no one else would;
and paid the price others fled
Hail Him,
Tyr.

Evening Rite for Tyr

This ritual is best done toward the end of the day. Begin by setting up an altar. Any images or items that you associated with Tyr are appropriate for the altar. Additionally, there should be a candle, and a glass of juice or alcohol to give in offering.

For Tyr, I always feel it appropriate to do some type of personal cleansing before entering into His ritual space. So I recommend doing this ritual toward the end of the day after bathing and changing clothes. It's good to change clothes anyway after a hard day's work – it helps the unconscious mind to well and truly unhook from one's working day.

Once you've prepared everything, including yourself, sit in front of your altar and center yourself for a few moments. When you feel ready, light the candle and offer the following prayer (you may also substitute a prayer of your own for this or any other prayer in these rites).

Invocation to Tyr

I hail Tyr, God of the law.
I hail the Warrior,
Wise in weapons-craft,
Who exchanged His honor
to bind the wolf.

I hail the God,
Who made the difficult choice,
because it was necessary
for the good of his people.

Hail Tyr,
when the difficult choices
come before me in my life,
may I have the courage
to make the necessary choices too.
I honor You this night.

Offering to Tyr

Sitting in front of the altar, contemplate the following: what is honor to you? What is your code of honor? This is not just a question for warriors, but for every single one of us. If you've never thought about this before (and many people haven't), then spend the next few Tyr's days thinking on it and seeing where you stand. It's a good question to revisit every so often, even if you have a clear sense of what your code of honor and ethics might be.

If you have thought this out and revisited it recently, spend this time, as long as you may need, going over your day. Think about where you lived up to the standards of behavior you set for yourself and where you fell short. Think about where you would like to improve, and think about those who inspire you. Think about how you will do better the following day.

When you are finished, pour the juice or alcohol that you have set aside into a glass and set it on the altar with the words, "I make this offering to You, Tyr. Please help me to walk the road of my life through each day rightly and well."

Meditation

Spend as long as you need in contemplation of honor, this God, and the story of His interactions with Fenris.

Closing Prayer

Thank You, Tyr,
for Your blessings.
May I walk through my day,
this day, tomorrow, and every other,
always mindful

of Your shining example of honor.

Hail, Tyr.

The ritual is now complete. You may allow the candle to burn down, or blow it out and save it for the next Tuesday night ritual.

Suggestions for Tyr

Colors: dark red, dark grey

Symbols: sword, hand imagery, weapons that are kept in good, working order, oath rings, holly tree (holly symbolizes the sacred warrior), the rune Tiewaz

Food and drink: mead, meat, bread. He is a soldier, assume he eats like a military man; in other words, anything (and I say this being the daughter and granddaughter of soldiers).

Service offerings: consider a donation to one of the following organizations: Disabled American Veterans (www.dav.org), Fisher House Foundation (www.fisherhouse.org), The Military Religious Freedom Foundation (www.militaryreligiousfreedom.org), The Wounded Warrior Project (www.woundedwarriorproject.org), American Women Veterans (www.americanwomenveterans.org), Paralyzed Veterans of America (www.pva.org); stand up against bullying in your schools; if you have children consider working with the school and/or PTA to educate and raise awareness; donate to a wolf sanctuary; protect or defend someone who is unable to protest him or herself; train in a weapons art or other martial art specifically as a devotional act to Tyr

Contraindicated: letting weapons get rusty or dirty; dishonorable behavior within the range of His space; breaking your sworn word; dishonoring or mistreating veterans; dishonoring or mistreating animals

WEDNESDAY: HONORING WODEN

It's such a joy to hail Him, like coming home. When it comes to make my daily offerings on Wednesday, which is Woden's Day, something deep and unspoken within my being relaxes. I can't explain it save that the heart knows its own.

People ask me all the time what type of rituals I do for Him. They're curious, I guess, about the specificities of my practice. The problem is, I don't have any. I rarely approach the Old Man with formalized rituals. In fact, unless I am facilitating a rite for someone else (which happens rarely) I feel somewhat silly being suddenly so formal with the God that knows me more intimately than any Other. I'll catch myself when I start the formal invocations thinking, "Why the hell am I being so formal?" Of course, that does not mean I am disrespectful. I don't want to give that impression. I hope that my work, my devotional practices, my life are all grounded in respect, love, and piety. I work toward that as a consistent goal. It's just hard to be formal with a God I love so much.

Some of my devotions to Him are almost unconscious. I do a lot of different things on Wednesday but it wasn't until I sat and thought about them that I realized how instinctual some of them have become. For instance, I tend to wear Woden's colors (blue, black, or grey) on Wednesdays – usually blue. It's a simple thing, a silly thing perhaps, but it calls Him to the forefront of my mind. It helps me feel connected as I go about my day. I often find myself sitting down to meditate on Him before I even realize it's His day. Of course this is not uncommon on other days too. Mostly I just cultivate a sense of His presence on Wednesdays, a sense that the very fabric of the day itself is permeated through and through with the essence of Him.

Of course, there's the regular offering of whiskey or aquavit, sometimes wine and quite often a bit of dark chocolate to go along with it. Often I will invoke Him before dinner and share a meal in His presence. In all ways, large and small, Wednesdays belong to Him. I find ways, even when I'm not thinking about it, to bring my awareness of His presence to the fore.

For now, praise Him.
Praise the passage of His storm.

Praise that which He tears away,
and that which He brings to fruition.
Praise His hunger.
Praise the terror He evokes.
Praise the ecstasy He may bring,
and the breath of His inspiration.
In all ways that can be spoken,
and even more those ways that can not
praise Him.
Woden.

Evening Rite for Woden

Begin as usual, by setting up a small altar for Woden. Anything that reminds you of Woden, or calls His canon of sacred stories to mind is appropriate. You should also have a candle, some incense, and either aquavit or whiskey to use as an offering and, if possible, a bit of tobacco. Have a glass for the alcohol and a small bowl for the tobacco (or ash tray if you're using a cigarette, tobacco, or pipe).

Sit in front of the altar and spend a few moments centering yourself. Then, turning your attention to Woden, light the candle and a bit of incense and offer the following prayer.

Invocation to Woden

Hail to Woden,
World-shaper, wisdom seeker,
Wyrd walker, wandering God.
Hail to He Who brings
both weal and woe
Who hung on the Tree,
Who gnawed upon His own spear,
to tear a hole between the worlds.
Hail to He, who won the runes,
Who, burned by their fire,
Shrieked His spells,
and burned them all right back.
Hail to the All-Father,

Ruthless, fearless, mighty God,
Weapons wise and wondrous Lord.
Bestow Your blessings upon me here tonight,
and may my prayer be pleasing to You.
Hail, Woden.

Meditation

In our cosmology, Woden (or Odin) is the God who breathed His breath into the first human beings, imbuing them with life. He's the breath-giver, and our continued breath is His gift. The first breath we take is drawn from Him and the last breath we exhale will be given back to Him. That is the focus of this meditation, that primal connection, that spiritual umbilicus.

Sitting comfortably, begin to focus on your breath. Feel the coolness of the breath as you inhale. Allow yourself to feel the intercostals (the muscles between your ribs) expand and release. Spend a few moments focusing on the inhalation, the feel of the breath flowing into your lungs, the expansion of your diaphragm followed by the exhalation, the rush of breath leaving your lungs, the contraction. Become aware of the circular rhythm and once you have spent a few moments focusing on your breath, turn your attention to Woden.

As you breathe, think about the creation story. Think about that first kiss of breath, the moment that Odin breathed life into Ask and Embla, waking them to their own humanity. Think about what that set in motion, and the long progression of humanity that flowed from the moment of that kiss.

Visualize, feel, or imagine (whatever works for you – people work and process these things differently and not everyone is visual) that you are connected to Woden by the cord of your breath, by that very rhythm of the inhalation and exhalation of your breathing. Imagine that as you inhale, you are consciously drinking in His breath, that He is breathing into you, and as you exhale, you are breathing into Him and He is drinking in your breath. Continue this for at least five minutes, longer if you can. Focus on the give and take, on drinking in His breath, and the connection further strengthened when you exhale into Him. When you are ready to stop, exhale for a final time and then take a few moments to re-orient yourself to your space, making sure that you are properly grounded.

Offering

Pour out some of the whiskey or aquavit into a glass and put it on the altar, offering it to Woden with the words, "Divine Breath-giver, I give this liquor to You in offering." Light the tobacco if it is a cigarette or cigar or pipe otherwise just sprinkle it into a small offering bowl. "I also give You this tobacco, for Your pleasure. May these small gifts be pleasing to You. Hail, Woden."

Closing Prayer

Thank You, Woden,
for Your wisdom.
I hail You now, All-Father,
and always.
Hail, Woden.

The ritual is now ended. You may allow the candle to burn down or, if you wish, snuff it out and save it for the next Wednesday night's rite.

Suggestions for Woden

Colors: Grey, deep cobalt blue, black
Symbols: valknot, spear, wolves, ravens
Stones: labradorite, black goldstone, lapis
Herbs and Trees: tobacco, the nine sacred herbs, ash leaves, elm leaves, parsley (associated with Wild Hunt), woad, cinquefoil, horehound, periwinkle
Runes: technically, all the runes are His, but specifically ansuz, othala, gebo, and wunjo
Food and drink: good quality alcohol (mead, dry red wine,

whiskey, cognac, and other hard liquor especially aquavit), smoked salmon, red meats, spearlike vegetables such as leeks, asparagus, and garlic

Service offerings: Woden is, in part, a God of warriors, so many of the same organizations to which one might donate for Tyr are appropriate for Odin as well; He is also a God of knowledge and education, so one might donate to an educational charity like www.donorschoose.org; He also has a role as a Healer, so one might consider Physicians for Human Rights (www.physiciansforhuman rights.org) or Doctors without Borders (www.doctorswithout borders.org); one could also reach out and help someone who is struggling to come into the faith, or volunteer to teach literacy; donating books to children or schools in need is also an appropriate offering

Contraindicated: cowardice, not 'sucking the marrow' out of one's experiences, shirking military service

THURSDAY: HONORING THOR

Thursday is Thor's day and He is perhaps one of our most popular Deities. That's true, by the way, both in the time of our polytheistic ancestors and in the contemporary community. Thor is the God of the common man, the protector of human kind and He helps to gird the world against dissolution and destruction. It's fitting, by the way, that He should have been given the day that falls right after Woden's, since He is Woden's son.

His hammer Mjolnir is a manifestation of His sacred might, of His power, the force that He is able to embody and utilize as part of His proffered protection. He not only guards Midgard, the human world, but He is also the Protector of Asgard. It does not hold, however, as some Heathens seem to think, that He just randomly goes around killing giants. He might kill a Jotun should that Jotun prove a threat but He is not a wanton killer of any race. In fact, quite often He takes counsel from Jotun women - perhaps something He learned from His father.

I think because His primary attribute is great physical strength, there's an unfortunate image of Thor as strong, but not too intellectually bright. I've never understood that. First of all, this is Odin's son we're talking about. He was fathered by the God of knowledge. Secondly, the surviving tales themselves don't bear this out. In the Eddic poem *Alvissmal*, Thor protects His daughter from the machinations of a scheming duergar named Alviss by means of a contest of wits. This is one of the reasons that He's called 'Deep-Minded.' I wanted to highlight this because all too often I've seen Him presented as the 'all brawn, no brains' type when nothing is further from the truth. Thor is every bit as wise as His father – wise enough to allow Himself to go underestimated, I might add.

In offerings, I have always found Thor to be fairly low key and down to earth. I pour Him a drink, usually whiskey, and set it out with a small prayer and that's it. Now, someone dedicated to Him, or someone with a deeper devotional relationship to Him than I might do more but I suspect He's pretty 'no frills' about these things as a matter of course. A plate of food – meat and potatoes type food, good sausage, things that 'stick to your ribs' as the saying goes – is a good offering too.

Hail Thor,
Protector of Midgard.
Hail Thor,
Mighty As.
Hail Thor,
Wise as His Father.
You bless Midgard with Your might.

Evening Rite for Thor
Begin by setting up an altar to Thor. Anything that summons His stories or presence to your mind is appropriate on the altar. If you have a ritual Thor's hammer, that is also appropriate to have on hand. Have a small bowl of grain and a glass of whiskey to give in offering. There should also be a candle.

Once you are ready, sit in front of your altar and spend a few moments centering yourself. Then light the candle and offer the following prayer:

Invocation to Thor

Hail Thor, God of Thunder!
Hail Odin's Son,
strong Protector of Mankind,
girding the Worlds from harm.

Hail Defender of Midgard,
Mighty Hammer Wielder!
Look kindly on me here.
Hail Your Strength
and hail Your power,
hail Your might,
and hail Your mien.
Hail Your compassion,
Hail Your wisdom
Pride of Asgard,
Odin's Son.
Hail mighty Thor!

Meditation

Settle yourself comfortably and think about power, your relationship to it, your emotional response to the idea and word. How do you claim and exercise power in your life? Are you comfortable doing so? What is power to you? What do you think the ethics of power might be? This concept is a particularly charged one in our culture. It's something from which women especially tend to shy. Can you visualize yourself directly and actively using power? Think about times that you have been involved in a power dynamic (and we are, all the time; every relationship in some way involves a power dynamic). When have you navigated that well, and when have you navigated it badly? How do you feel when you envision yourself wielding power, or being in a subordinate position to it? How would you wield power rightly and well? Could you? What power dynamics did you engage in during the day, and what were the results both positive and negative?

When you are satisfied that you have examined this situation at length, turn your attention to making your offering.

Offering

Pour out a glass of juice or alcohol and lay out whatever other offerings you have prepared with the words, "I offer these gifts to you, mighty Thor. Thank you for Your blessings and Your protection. May these small gifts of thanks be pleasing."

Closing Prayer

Thank you, Thor,
for Your care and Your protection.
Thank You great Defender of Midgard.
May You always be hailed.

The ritual is now over. You may allow the candle to burn down, or snuff it out and save it for next Thursday's rite. The offerings may be disposed of the following morning.

Suggestions for Thor

Colors: sky blue, red, sometimes green and gold
Symbols: hammer, goats, belt and gloves of strength, thunder
Altar suggestions: Thor's hammer figures, model goats (ideally pulling a cart), weapons, shield, metal lightning bolts
Herbs and plants: garlic, leek, onion, hawthorn, houseleek, tormentil, oak, rowen
Food and drink: mead, beer, goat, hearty foods with large amounts of meat
Service offerings: donate time to an organization dedicated to protecting children or women from abuse; help someone move, or do some other sort of heavy work for someone in need of it; donate

to an organization that cares for climate and environment – because He is associated with storms, I suggest The Wind Works Project (www.thewindworksproject.com)

Contraindicated: pieces of flint or knife whetstones, meat with broken bones in it (large pieces of meat can be jointed, but the bones should not be cut or broken)

FRIDAY: HONORING FRIGGA AND FREYA

There is some disagreement on which Deity governs Friday. I believe etymologically, the day belongs to Frigga, but some people claim Freya as well. In my household devotions, I tend to split the difference and honor Them both on this day. I also usually honor Sigyn on this day because I love Her and because I like to include Her as much as possible in my regular devotions. Again, as with the other Deities honored in this weekly cycle, my offerings aren't elaborate: a glass of wine, perhaps a bit of incense or flowers. That's all. I'll offer a respectful prayer when I make my offerings but the hallmark of this weekly cycle is its simplicity. It's a very, very easy thing to integrate into one's daily life. For people who are just coming into the tradition, who don't know very much about the Gods but who really want to get started developing a devotional practice, following the weekly cycle can be a very good and solid place to begin.

Of all the Deities that I honor, I am perhaps at my most formal with Frigga. There are those who have said to me, or insinuated, that as a godspouse of Odin I am attempting to set myself up as Frigga's equal. To that, I can only respond: absolutely not! To do such a thing would be blasphemy. There are others who assume I must have a contentious relationship with Her but that is also not the case. I respect Frigga immensely. 'Godspouse' is the best word that I have in the languages with which I'm familiar for the most intimate part of my relationship with Odin. It in no way comes close to anything He might have with another Deity. It is a completely different thing, as the devotional experience between human and Deity must, by its very nature, be different. It does not even approximate what He has with Frigga and no godspouse that I know of would attempt to imply that it does.

So why am I so formal with Her? Well, there is something about Her nature that evokes it from me. I tend to be sensitive to power dynamics and She is a Goddess of power. Frigga is a power-broker. She is like the CEO and COO of Asgard combined! She is a Goddess in complete control of everything around Her. She exudes power and in the presence of that, I revert automatically and instinctually to a very formal protocol. I am far more likely to cleanse myself, clean the area of Her altar, possibly even the entire room, and cover my head before approaching Her altar. These are things I usually do before major rituals.

Moreover, as a diviner, part of my ancestor shrine is given over to honoring my lineage ancestors (those who preceded me in the work of divination, those who were shamans before me, those who were priests of the Gods before me). I keep an image of Frigga there as patron of that shrine. She is a Goddess Who sees and knows all but keeps her silence. I petition Her to help me honor my lineage ancestors wisely and well, and to help me give clean, honorable service. What all this means is that with Frigga, I 'mind my Ps and Qs!'

With Freya, it's a different story. I have a shrine to Freya in my bedroom. I'm very informal in my offerings to Her – respectful always, but far less formal than the way in which I approach Frigga. Part of it is that it took me many years to develop a devotional relationship with Her. My impression from within that relationship now is that She wants me to be relaxed and not to stress about engaging with Her. There were times when it was a struggle after all. But someone else might have a completely different experience or may even find their response to these two magnificent Goddesses is precisely reversed. That's just how it works sometimes. Each relationship is different.

Freya is a Goddess of power too, of abundance and wealth, of sexuality, sex, attraction, and eroticism, and of witchcraft and magic. She defers to no one. She is also a Goddess of war. It's a toss up as to whether She or Frigga is our most loved Goddess but I think I can safely say that They are both very well revered within Heathenry.

I tend to collect non-edible offerings to Her (usually amber, jewelry, incenses, etc.) throughout the year and then at Beltane or Summer Solstice dispose of them in a sacred bonfire. By January and February of any given year, the altar can be a bit cluttered. I've never had the zen of keeping things sparse and balanced and neat! Still, every Friday, I bring Her a glass of wine, usually something sweet. Sometimes, I'll buy small bottles of goldschlager for Her. Sometimes a good Gewürztraminer.

I have found in honoring Freya that She demands that respect be given to all the areas that She governs. That includes sex and sexuality. One may not scorn the beauty and power of the flesh and remain in Her good graces — at least that has been my observation. That's not always easy. I have found that for most of us it's easier to blame what makes us uncomfortable than to accept that the issues causing the discomfort are our own. For instance, Freya is a Goddess of sexual pleasure. Period. That includes heterosexual, homosexual and everything in between. It includes monogamous and polyamorous, it includes self love. It may include BDSM; it may include the most vanilla of sexual pleasures. Somewhere in all of that there's something that will make someone freak the fuck out. That doesn't mean whatever that might be is wrong. It means we all have our issues and the adult thing to do is own them.

This is was a huge hurdle for me in honoring Freya for a very long time. But one cannot honor a Deity and scorn that Deity's gifts. I found that in my struggles, asking Freya for help was the best medicine I could possibly find. The Gods are not insensitive to our struggles and if it is not blocked by our own wyrd, if it is permitted, They are usually willing to help when and where They can. Even when something is blocked, there is an offering for everything. Many a door can be opened with the proper devotion.

One day, I shall write adorations for both Frigga and Freya, but for now, these brief prayers shall have to whet my readers' appetites.

I adore You, Frigga, Queen of Asgard.
I adore You, Frigga, Power Broker.
I adore You, Frigga, Beloved of Odin.
I adore You, Frigga, Mother of Baldr.
I adore You, Frigga, Who drives back disorder.
I adore You, Frigga, Mighty Seer.
I adore You, Frigga, more cunning than Your Husband.
Hail Frigga, now and always.

I adore You, Freya, Mighty Lady of the Vanir.
I adore You, Freya, bold in battle.
I adore You Freya, Who defers to no one.
I adore You, Freya, Desire of the Worlds.
I adore You, Freya, Secure in Your Power.
I adore You, Freya, Goddess of Passion.
I adore You, Freya, Giver of Gifts.
Hail Freya, ever Magnificent.
Hail Freya, always.

Evening Rite for Frigga and Freya
 Set up a small altar to both of these Goddesses. When you are
ready, sit or stand in front of it and begin your ritual.

Invocation to Frigga

Shining Lady of Asgard,
All-seeing, All-knowing,
at Your command worlds are born,
at Your nod, life bursts into being.

You are a valiant Goddess, ruthless Foe,
a cunning Queen, Who with Your wise maneuvering
even bested Odin in His games – more than once.

Great Lady, please hear my prayer.
Illuminate my wyrd, that I may craft it rightly.
Strengthen my hamingja and grant me clarity of spirit.

Teach me to be strong in my purpose
that I may honor the Gods rightly and well.

Holy Mother, Power of Fensalir,
Grant me Your blessing,
and I will always honor You.

Hail Frigga.

Invocation to Freya

Hail to the Lady of amber.
Hail to the Lady of steel.
Hail to the Lady of passion,
Bringer of luck,
Bestower of wealth.
You are the envy of all the Gods,
the treasure of the nine sacred worlds.

Freya, mighty and magnificent,
I praise Your name with my Passions.
Ignite within me an awareness
of my own creative fire.
Ignite within me hunger,
to burn through the pale shadows of my life
and to find integrity:
in all I do, in all I dream, in all I am.
Bless me, Freya, Lady of the Vanir,
and I shall hail You,
always.

Offering

Light two candles and set out a glass of white wine for Frigga
and a glass of Goldschlager or rum for Freya. If you are not of legal
drinking age, juice is okay. If you are on a very tight budget, there
is nothing wrong with giving water. As you do so, ask for Their
blessings.

Meditation

Both of these Goddesses deal with power. They're power brokers and their core competencies involve the careful use of power. Consider how you relate to power, authority (including being in a position of authority), and hierarchy. What feelings do these things evoke in you? If you have ever had to supervise someone, how did you feel about that? How did it go? Positive use of power is necessary for building a tradition, protecting a community, governance, resource management. Think about how Frigga and Freya both exemplify this. Consider how you could engage with power more effectively and in a healthier manner. When you are finished, thank Them and conclude with the following prayer.

Closing Prayer

Thank You, Frigga.
Thank You, Freya.
For Your protection,
and Your strength,
for the order and passion
You each bring to the world,
I am grateful.
Hail Frigga.
Hail Freya.

Suggestions for Frigga

Colors: white, ivory, blue
Symbols: spindle, spun wool, hearth, birth tree, geese, keys
Altar suggestions: traditional Norse style spindle, white wool carded or spun, spinning equipment including small replicas of spinning wheels, a bunch of old-fashioned keys, goose feathers, the rune berkana
Herbs: birch wood and leaves, rosemary, borage, lady's mantle,

thyme, weld

Food and drink: organic milk, mead, pastry, light, fruity wines, Riesling

Service offerings: help mothers and children; make peace between warring members of a group; clean your house or someone else's (particularly if you know someone who is too ill or injured to do so); help someone get organized; comfort the grieving; consider a donation to one of these charities: IPAS: Protecting Women's Healthcare (www.ipas.org), The Emeril Lagasse Foundation (www.emeril.org), Jamie Oliver Foundation (www.jamieoliver.com/foundation), or Kiva (www.kiva.org)

Contraindicated: letting the altar area get dirty; not maintaining one's house or household accounts properly

Suggestions for Freya

Colors: this really depends on which aspect of Freya you're calling upon: fertility Goddess: green; love Goddess: rose and gold, warrior: white and red; seidhrkona: deep purple grey, Mardoll: pearly white, ocean blue and shimmering hues in the color of sand

Symbols: cats (some say wolverines, weasels, or lynxes instead of domestic felines), gold and amber, necklaces to symbolize Brisingamen, heart-shaped stones and charms, blades

Altar suggestions: figures of cats, particularly gold and orange ones, furs of cats, lynxes, weasels, wolverines, falcon feathers, amber, amber, and more amber, gold, flowers, the rune fehu

Herbs: linden, beans, daisy, cowslip, primrose, lily-of-the-valley, damiana, rose

Food and drink: sweet wine or mead, sweet pastries, strawberries (particularly if they're drenched in honey), Goldschlager, high quality expensive wine, high quality chocolate, marzipan, high quality organic honey

Service offerings: give aid to someone who represents one of Freya's aspects: a young woman trying to get pregnant, an unmarried maiden, a woman warrior, a sex worker, a seidhr-worker (one of Freya's lessons is knowing one's own worth; whenever you can help another young woman to learn to value herself, to learn the measure of her worth, this is pleasing to Freya); donate time to a rape crisis counseling center; donate time to keeping contraception and abortion safe, accessible, and legal; consider donating to one of these organizations: IPAS: Protecting Women's Healthcare (www.ipas.org) or Planned Parenthood (www.plannedparenthood. org) or American Women Veterans (www.americanwomen veterans.org)

Contraindicated: Ugly things (Goddesses of love, sex and beauty like aesthetic beauty as a general rule); no food offering should be left to get stale or rot or mold; flowers should be removed as soon as they are no longer fresh; obviously disrespecting women is not pleasing to Freya

SATURDAY: HONORING LOKI

Saturday is weird. It's the one day wherein the name that's come down to us pulls not from Heathen traditions but from Rome. Saturday really means Saturn's Day and obviously Saturn was not a Norse Deity! To the Norse tribes, as far as I've been able to tell, Saturday was a day for cleaning. Specifically, it was a day to do your laundry and take a bath. This amuses me. It didn't amuse Viking Age Christians though. Complaints have come down to us from Viking Age English chronicles of Christians whining that the Vikings got all the ladies — because they bathed once a week, combed their hair, and washed their clothes. Heaven forfend!

Rest assured, I bathe everyday not just on Saturday! Instead, I use Saturday partly to clean my altars and shrines. When you have a lot of them it's painfully easy to let them go a bit too long between cleanings. I make it a point to clean at least five or six of them each Saturday and then I just rotate out Saturday by Saturday until they're all clean. Then the cycle starts again.

I also use Saturday as a day specifically to honor Loki and Sigyn. Long ago when I started following this weekly cycle of offerings, I decided that since Saturday was a 'free' day insofar as offerings went, I was free to ascribe it to any Deity I wanted. It made sense to me, since I love Them dearly, to add Loki and Sigyn to my weekly rotation. Besides, the grace notes of domesticity are something that I very strongly associate with Sigyn. She knows how to maintain a space, how to keep it so clean that nothing negative or malignant can find any purchase at all. On a spiritual level, being clean in one's motivations and free of miasma are essential qualities.

So on Saturdays, I pour out offerings to Sigyn and Her Husband. I maintain several shrines to Them both in my home: the first is downstairs in my foyer, just as one enters my home and this is where I leave offerings to Them. This a shared shrine: both Loki and Sigyn have Their space there and there's a framed image of Them plus Their sons Narvi and Vali hanging right above. I leave glasses of wine, whiskey, and often milk and bread for Sigyn. If I have any chocolate or candy in the house, I'll usually give some of that as well. I put out offerings to these two Deities quite frequently, not just on Saturdays, because I have an ongoing devotional practice to both of Them, but even so I make it a special point to put offerings out on Saturdays too, regardless of what I have given Them the rest of the week.

I like that there is a day worked into the Norse week devoted to cleansing. Of course we want to be clean physically but it's also fundamental on an energetic and spiritual level. It sets the stage for doing authentic work with integrity. That's no small thing.

Hail Sigyn,
Goddess of the Staying Power.
Goddess of small things
that in the end aren't so small.
Help me to love You
rightly and well.
Help me to be clean
in my work.

Hail Loki,
Husband of Sigyn.

Let me never lose sight
of the joy that can be found
in the intricacies
of devotion.

Hail Loki, Hail Sigyn.

Saturday Ritual for Loki

Begin by setting up an altar to Loki. When you are ready, take a
few moments to center yourself and then begin this rite.

Invocation to Loki

I praise the best-born Son of Jotunheim,
Sigyn's Secret Sweetness.
I praise this God who gnaws on courage,
spitting forth truth though some may call Him Father of Lies.
I praise the Flame-haired Sky-Treader,
with His brilliant mind and cunning tongue,
and that wit – most wondrous of weapons.
I praise His tenderness, and His kindness,
He who turned female to bear Svadilfari's son.
I praise His passion, His love, His commitment.
Most of all we praise Him, Loki, for Himself alone.
May You be hailed in all Your magnificence, with all of our joy,
on this day and each day forward.

Offerings

Light a candle on your shrine and make an offering of drink to
Him.

Meditation

Sit and meditate in prayer to Loki for as long as you wish, then
get up and clean your household shrines. Since Saturday was a
cleaning day for the Norse, I can think of no better way to honor
Loki than to incorporate that into your daily meditation. On a
purely practical level it will also force you to keep your shrines

clean! When you are finished, thank Him and offer the following closing prayer.

Closing Prayer

I thank You, Loki,
for keeping me honest,
for forcing me to face
my own prejudice, my own
dark, twisting, rotten parts,
and for showing me how
to drag them into the light.
Hail, Loki.

Suggestions for Loki

Colors: Red, orange, gold, some Loki's folk see blue (the hottest part of the flame is blue)

Symbols: fox, crow, flame, spider, flea, fly, salmon, seal, the rune dagaz

Altar suggestions: candle or lamp, net, spider web, interesting or humorous toys, tricky puzzles, hot herbs, particularly peppers, the runes dagaz, kenaz and sometimes os and raido, hearts (He loves those He loves so very fiercely), basalt

Herbs: hot herbs, alder, mullein, celandine

Food and drink: strong liquor, candy, very spicy food, any food with intense flavor that gives you a rush (some people report giving Him Tang and marshmallow Peeps), anything you happen to be eating – share your food with Him

Service offerings: do something difficult without expectation of reward or thanks (whenever you do a thankless task that needs to be done, you are doing Loki's work); strive to speak truthfully, most especially with yourself; speak out against injustice and hypocrisy; make an offering to Sigyn; make an offering to any of His children

Contraindicated: don't put His altar next to Skadhi's or Heimdall's; do not speak ill of Sigyn or His children; do not behave like an ass in His name.

SUNDAY: HONORING SUNNA, GODDESS OF THE SUN

Sunday is dedicated to the Sun Goddess Sunna. To those steeped in Greek and Roman sacred stories, the idea of a Sun Goddess might seem every bit as strange as a moon God, but it was not uncommon in Indo-European influenced cultures. You find it in Lithuania too, and Egypt, and even -- though it's not indo-European – Japan.

I'm not much of a morning person. I've always preferred late evening when most people are asleep and the psychic white noise of their ever chattering consciousnesses is finally silent – more or less. Daytime means having to put on my 'Midgard drag' as I like to call it, and brave the crowded world again with all the psychic shielding that entails. Really, I'd rather sleep in.

Still, day brings with it Sunna's magnificence and that is a gift and a glory worth hauling oneself out of bed to experience. She is our sun Goddess, sometimes called Sol, and She blazes across the heavens just like Her brother Mani and yet so very different.

If I were more of a morning person, I would rise early and sit on my porch in order to watch Her drive back the darkness of night, the very fabric of the grey curtain of evening rolling itself back before Her gleaming chariot. It truly is something to see. I'm not a morning person though, so instead I drag myself out later in the morning and make offerings, usually of wine to Her with simple prayers – as coherent as I can muster upon first waking. Sometimes I wait until the evening when I can make my offerings with more mindfulness. Then I will spend more time in prayer.

We don't talk much about Sunna (and Mani) in contemporary Heathenry but the majority of our ancestors lived agrarian lives. They lived and died by Sunna's grace. We do today too, we just don't realize it as readily because few of us are living bound directly to the land. We still depend on the fruits of the land though to nourish us and our families. We still depend on Sunna. When Sunna ceases to drive Her chariot across the sky the earth will cease to be in any way livable. That's worth considering now and again. Sunna's labors further life on our planet, are essential to it. The least we can do is pour out an offering to Her once a week.

Hail Sunna,
mighty Pacesetter.
Hail the Goddess
Who drives Her gleaming chariot across darkened skies,
bringing light, bringing warmth, bringing the grace of morning.
Hail Sunna,
Protector of our ancestors,
Who brought health
and the bounty of a good harvest.
Sister of Mani,
blazing Goddess of life-giving Power,
Hail.

Morning Rite to Sunna

Begin by setting up an altar to Sunna. Better yet, if you are able,
do this one outside.

Invocation to Sunna

Hail the rising of the Sun.
Great Goddess, Bestower of all good things,
shining brightly You traverse the heavens
driving back the blanket of night.

Mighty Sunna, be my pace-setter.
Help me to structure my day rightly,
with time to work, and play, and pray.

Let me not lose myself in the hammering call
of all that has to be done.
Help me to follow Your rhythms,
for You are wise and practical
and Your presence blesses us all.

Hail, Sunna.

Offerings

Pour out good strong alcohol, cider, applejack, mead, organic juice, or water to Her and ask Her blessings. Perhaps bring an offering of fresh fruit as well.

Meditation

Go outside and stand in the sunlight, or stand in the window where you can experience the warmth and light of the sun. Practice the four-fold centering breath for a few moments, then begin to imagine that you are inhaling and breathing in Her warmth and light. With each inhalation you are more fully filled with these things until you are over flowing. Continue this as long as you need then thank Sunna for Her blessings.

Closing Prayer

I give thanks to You, Sunna,
for Your blessings:
vitality, strength, growth,
abundance, for being our
Pace-setter,
for forging
a blazing trail
across the sky.
May You be ever hailed.

Suggestions for Sunna

Colors: golds, oranges, reds, greens
Symbols: anything shaped like the sun or with the sun on it, sunwheel images, sunflowers, horse drawn chariots, green, growing things, the rune sowelo or dagaz
Stones: sunstone, orange quartz, citrine, amber
Food and drink: Goldschlager, cider, mead, apple juice
Flowers: sunflowers, plants, fruits (especially citrus and apples)
Other offerings: gold, any work which benefits the land or works

toward helping the environment; any work that makes you more mindful of your own health; consider donating to one of the following charities: Doctors without Borders (www.doctorswithout borders.org), The Big Sur Land Trust (www.bigsurlandtrust.org), Scenic Hudson (www.scenichudson.org), or The Wind Works Project (www.thewindworksproject.com)

Contraindicated: egregiously showing disrespect for land, air, and environment

Holy Tides:
Marking the Year with the Gods

The following is a collection of articles that I have written over the past several years on the Holy Tides, the holy days of the Heathen calendar.

IMBOLC/CHARMING OF THE PLOUGH

Poet T.S. Elliot called April the cruelest month, but I've always thought February fits that appellation far more thoroughly and resolutely. I detest this month, though I have to admit that it wasn't always so. My adopted mom died in February, though, and since then everything – from the snow and ice, to Valentine's Day decorations, to the joyful celebrations of Chinese New Year – reminds me of her passing. For me, it's turned an otherwise innocuous month into something bleak and grim. Still, there are bright spots: Chinese New Year for one. The child in me adores the decorations and yearly animal signs and my household usually holds some type of celebration to honor the Lunar New Year and that brightens the month considerably. The other things I look forward to are the celebrations of Imbolc and Charming of the Plough. Even though I'm Heathen, I tend to celebrate both, partly in homage to my Celtic ancestors, partly because February needs all the holiday help it can get!

Imbolc (or Candlemas) is a feast of lights, traditionally given to the Goddess Brigid, and it celebrates the slow turning of the seasons away from the woe of winter's cold into the brightness of spring and summer. It celebrates the return of light, and the lengthening of days that inevitably follows the solstice. Charming of the Plough, celebrated in February as well, often incorporates a blessing of the fields and, with the slow march toward spring, honors the coming readiness of the land to accept plowing and planting. Both are celebrations of potential, potentiality, and massive creativity and drive. In contemporary Heathenry, since most of us no longer make our livelihood directly from working the land, it is not uncommon to bring pens and laptops, work proposals, craft projects, and tools of one's particular trade to be blessed on this day. It's a time to honor creativity in all its facets, particularly and most importantly the harnessing of the creative force in all those ways that enable us to sustain ourselves and to nourish our families.

In a way, that's what these holidays are about: how do we find sustenance in the modern world? How do we provide for our families? Is our work something honorable and healthy? Does it nourish us spiritually and emotionally as well as providing necessary cash-flow? Creativity is sacred. What outlets do we allow ourselves for creative expression? How do we craft our wyrd, our lives, our relationships? Imbolc and Charming of the Plough are about all of these things, these soul-questions that are far easier asked than answered. It's a chance to examine one's priorities and set new goals, or evaluate progress made toward the realization of dearly held passions. Perhaps it is a time to make offerings and pray that one finds one's passion.

There is a momentum in spring, and these holidays call us to consider how best we shall harness that momentum in our own lives. Now is the time for transformation; now the time to welcome in the blessings of regeneration and renewal that the Deities of this time and season can so readily bring. After all, in the scope of spiritual life, we block ourselves more thoroughly than any external foe could ever do. The fire of this season, consciously honored, gives us a powerful chance to partner with ourselves instead of fighting every step of the way. It allows us an opportunity to consciously choose right balance, right relationship: with the Gods, ancestors, with the land around us, with our communities, our families, and perhaps most of all with ourselves. It is a time of celebration and a time to renew one's commitment to all of those in our lives and that includes oneself.

Brigid, so intimately associated with Imbolc, is a Goddess of healing but She's also a Goddess of smithcraft. She is a consummate craftsman and many of Her lessons, there for anyone who takes the time to seek them out, speak to the nature of craft and the care, patience, and perseverance necessary to acquire excellence. One other thing our Deities of the forge – from Brigid, to Andvari, even to Wayland – teach: there is no greater craft that we as humans will ever touch or engage in, than the careful crafting of our wyrd. That is our highest art and we can craft our wyrd well by striving to live rightly and honorably, maintaining balance and the integrity of an honest piety, each and every day of our lives. We do that by paying attention to the details, because the wise craftsman knows that it's not the great things that matter, but the minutiae of the work day after day, that leads to the magnificence of the finished piece of art. There's so much in our lives that we cannot control. We can control this, however: our responses, our choices, the way we live in and navigate our world and everyone within it. Imbolc speaks to those connections and how we choose to maintain them or not. It's a time for reevaluation.

It is also a time to honor the blessings of fire. Our ancestors depended on fire for survival. From our most ancient past when they huddled in caves around a fire kindled not only for warmth, but also to keep predators at bay, to the founding of villages, towns, and cities dependant on fire for the cultivation of craft, the cooking of food, and the transformation of the gifts of earth into gifts of beauty through the heat of forge and furnace, our ancestors partnered with fire and in turn were blessed with the these things: cooking, glass blowing, smithcraft, jewelry making, and a thousand other arts – the grace notes of civilization. More importantly, fire brought warmth in the winter, and temporary stilling of the deathly grip of winter's cold. Our ancestors depended upon its mercy. It is our earliest ally, and one of our eldest ancestors – for in Norse cosmology at least, all life sprang from fire and ice.

So, too, Charming of the Plough teaches us not only to honor creativity and craft, but to honor that which sustains us. In the time of our ancestors, that was, more often than not, the land itself. We are taught to honor the land for its bounty, to pour out offerings in thanks and in hope. We are reminded that we are partners, not owners, to the land from which we draw sustenance. We are reminded of the blessing of work and all that it brings. We can use the momentum of these holidays to reconnect with our ancestors, and the depth and wisdom of those traditions we struggle each and every day not only to uphold, but to further. As our ancestors poured milk and honey into the frosty soil to honor the Earth Goddess Erda, to seek Her blessing on the crops that would in the months to come follow, so we too can say thank you to those people that nourish us in our lives: friends, family, even colleagues, maybe even our ancestors and Gods. We can honor those sometimes tenuous ties that sustain our world and enable us to find some measure of hope and comfort in the midst of our work.

Most of all, these holy tides also call us to joy. It is not a thing that Heathen lore speaks of often, but starting with the first blush of the coming spring, with the first courageous buds that choose to dare the winter's bite, with the slow but sure return of the green, we are called to joy. As much as there is horror and sadness, struggle and pain in living our lives in Midgard (the human world), so too there is the potential for tremendous kindness, beauty, and joy. We are called to remember these things, to seek them out, to laugh and love, and find our own grace notes of living. We are called to celebration and that is no small thing at all.

OSTARA

As winter slowly, seemingly unwillingly begins to release its hold on our world, many of us turn our minds to preparations for the upcoming holy tide of Ostara or Eostre. It's a welcome celebration after the grim cold and snow of winter, a time to rejoice in the blessings and renewal of spring. We don't know much about how our ancestors celebrated their holy days, but we do know that they honored this one. I suspect, given the harshness of the Northern winters, that spring equinox was a particularly welcome holiday. When we consciously honor this day, celebrate and hail our Gods, we are walking in the footsteps of our ancestors and that is a good and blessed thing.

We really don't have many references to Ostara/Eostre in the lore. The Anglo-Saxon scholar Bede mentions it briefly in *de Temporibus Ratione*, and it's mentioned again in the *Heimskringla*. Here we learn that the people were very persistent in celebrating this Pagan holiday and that sacrifices were customarily made to welcome spring and summer. Actually, we should realize that this was a relatively important holiday anyway because so many of its symbols and customs were co-opted by Christianity. Religions, after all, don't evolve in a vacuum and habitually cannibalize each other – and rabbits and eggs have nothing to do with Jesus. Still, with its emphasis on rebirth and renewal, Eostre was a good time to place the celebration of His resurrection, as these things go.

Christians renamed this celebration 'Easter' but the original name of this holiday comes from the name of a Goddess: Ostara or Eostre (the difference is a regional one with Eostre being the Anglo-Saxon version of the Norse name). The month in which this holiday falls was even known as 'Eostre-monath' or 'Eostre-month.' We know even less about this Goddess than we know about traditional customs of the holiday. For some, She is the embodiment of spring; for others, a Goddess of sunrise and the dawn. I have even known of some to ascribe to Her the aurora borealis (though I personally see this far more with the Goddess Gerda). I suppose in the end, it does not matter, so long as She is honored. This particular month and time of year is also associated with another little known Goddess, Hreðe, and tangentially with Erda, the earth Mother.

In honor of this holiday, I am going to be discussing two of these very special Goddesses, both of Whom are rarely well-honored today. As we move forward in the renewal and restoration of our traditions, this is an opportunity to also restore and renew the cultus of little-known Deities. We've lost so much. Make this your Ostara offering: choose a Deity of Whom almost nothing is known and honor Them. Seek Them out. Meditate on Their mysteries. Set up an altar to Them. Pray for inspiration. This is the way we will restore Their worship. This is the only way that we will fill in those gaps of knowledge because our ancestors did not rely on the written word for the transmission of their lore and precious little has come down to us first hand.

How else should one prepare for Ostara? Well, my mother would have to clean the house. There's a reason that we often refer to 'spring cleaning.' This is a time to make space, to remove clutter, to welcome in the free flow of energy, the emergence of the new after the inertia of winter. This is a time to pour out offerings into the land that it may be fruitful, to plant a garden, to greet the sun with joy. I know of one Heathen group that traditionally plants trees in March, usually on the actual Spring Equinox, as an offering to Ostara, and I think that is a lovely custom. In fact, it's an excellent time to make special offerings to the land vaettir, offerings of gratitude, respect, and acknowledgement.

In my neighborhood, many people create 'egg trees.' They hang plastic Easter eggs on any small trees in their yards. They do this for Easter, but it's a fitting custom for Ostara too and best of all, like having an Easter egg hunt on Ostara proper, it's something that can be enjoyed by children as well as adults. In fact, this is one of our holidays that is particularly enjoyable for kids. The egg and rabbit are traditional symbols of Ostara/Eostre because they are symbols of rebirth, renewal, and most of all fertility. I see nothing wrong with giving a bit of sweetness in the form of an Easter basket to Heathen and Pagan children. These symbols charm them and make the holiday fun and I think it's important that children find enjoyment in the celebration of our holy tides.

As Charming of the Plough honors the tools that work the land, Ostara honors the fecundity of the land itself. Here we taste the beginning of that vibrant sexual energy that reaches its apex at Walpurgis or Beltane. I suspect that ritual methods of drawing on and channeling this energy were one of the mysteries of Eostre that we have lost. This is a time to honor the hunger of flesh for flesh, the urge to procreate, the draw of one body to another. This is part of Her mysteries and as the holiday of Ostara is about the reawakening of the land, so too it is about the reawakening of the body's hungers: a celebration of carefully channeled spring fever!

We can also honor the moon God Mani and the Sun Goddess Sunna on Ostara because this is a day of balance, when night is equal to day. We're only just seeing the restoration of the worship of these two Deities, though Their importance to our ancestors, who despite tales of Viking raids lived largely agrarian lifestyles, was probably tremendous. Their blessings, after all, are necessary for any fecundity of the land.

The rabbit or hare has a long history as a sacred animal. The earliest known reference in British lore that comes to mind is Boudicca. Before going on her attacks against the Romans, she loosed a hare in honor of the Goddess Andraste. Further, the rabbit is a symbol of fecundity and fertility. The rabbit is also associated with the moon and was thought in many folklores to be a symbol of good luck. Rabbit is all about tapping into one's creativity, overcoming fear, and engaging in artistic expression – all good ways to herald in the spring!

We no longer live lives so intimately connected to the land as those of our ancestors yet we are still, in so many ways, dependent on those ancient rhythms for our health, state of mind, and yes, for sustenance. Though most of us aren't farmers, we still have to eat and despite all the inventions and interventions of modernity, that food still comes from the blessings of the earth. It is right and proper to honor its rhythms and to celebrate the turning of the seasonal tides so that we may continue reclaiming our traditions.

In addition to Eostre, there is an Anglo-Saxon Goddess also associated with this time of year: Hreðe. This Goddess holds a very special place in my heart for no other reason than that I was born at the tail end of Her month, March. We don't know very much about Her, other than that March is Her month and was once called 'Hreðe-monath' by our Anglo-Saxon forebears. Bede tells us this in his *de Temporibus Ratione*. Etymologically, Her name may mean 'the Victorious One' or 'the Famous One.' Beyond that, there's nothing but our willingness to seek Her out. Now granted, that's no small thing, however much we might wish for more concrete information. Still, many Heathens would give much to have a little more first-hand source material for Her worship.

Personally, I know this Goddess by feel, by the pressing momentum that for me so defines Her presence. When I sense Her, I sense also a tumble of rushing winds, a gaiety, and a fierceness. I associate Her with those brisk winds and I can't help but think of the old saying about March: "in like a lion, out like a lamb." She is best personified by the chill weather heralding and preceding the coming of spring. Given the etymology of Her name, there is some indication that She might have been a battle Goddess. Certainly She is a Goddess Who can really shake things up – not a bad thing, especially after the enforced inertia of winter. Being an Aries myself, I like to think that perhaps She can be said to embody the best characteristics of the Arien personality: independence, forcefulness, fearlessness, immense creative drive, catalytic power, and a certain whimsical attractiveness.

Scholar Rudolf Simek points to the world of folklorist Jakob Grimm and draws a connection between Hreðe and the Roman God Mars, which would reinforce both Her connection to battle, and Her connection to the land's fertility (Mars was originally a God of agriculture and fecundity of the land).

I usually honor Her in early March, and again when the sun passes into Aries. Chilly, windy days where the scent of spring is in the air but its promise not yet realized are perfect days to call Her name, pour out offerings, and honor the feel of Her presence. So this March, consider setting up an altar to Her, perhaps holding a ritual in Her honor. We are never going to adequately restore the traditions of our ancestors if we are unwilling to engage with the Holy Powers directly. For every Deity Whose name and ways of worship we know, another has been lost to us. Let's make sure that's not the case with Hreðe.

Prayer to Hreðe

I say hail to Hreðe, Mighty Goddess!
With explosive force, You banish winter.
With enervating drive, You push us into
the rejuvenating arms of Spring.
Cleanse me, Glorious Goddess,
of all those things that hold me back.
Unfetter my mind, heart, and will,
that I might set my feet unswervingly on the road
to victory.
Hail, Hreðe, ever-victorious in every struggle!

Prayer to Hreðe from an Aries child

The lion winds of March herald Your passing,
Victorious One,
Untamable, Fierce, and Proud:
You come, unstoppable, opening the way
for the gifts Eostre will soon bring.
You will not be bound.
You are as impossible to grasp
to hold, to contain
as the rushing winds
that so define this season.

When You come to me, oh Goddess,
it is with a pushing, driving momentum
that I can neither resist nor deny.
When Your presence fills my world,
it brings strength and laughter
and the whisper that something better
lies just around the corner,
if only I can run fast enough
to claim it, if only I don't give up.

I, born in the month of the ram—
Aries child, with temper and wit to match
that mighty sign's fearsome reputation,
I pay homage to You.
If it be not hubris, I like to think,
that perhaps You laughed,
on the day of my birth.

Please watch over me, Goddess,
of a month both raw and wild;
watch over this warrior child,
who strives always to be strong like You;
and I will praise Your name
always.

Ways to Honor Hreðe

Colors: light yellow, light blue, white – all colors I associate with the wind

    Symbols and Altar suggestions: streamers, lamb, ram, lion, pinwheels (like streamers, something that catches and plays in the wind), spring flowers, dandelions

Food and Drink offerings: good liquor, good wine, candy, cake and other sweets, spicy foods, mint juleps, mojitos (the common thread being mint)

Service offerings: make a donation to a charity like The Wind Works Project (www.thewindworksproject.com) that is devoted to clean air, reducing carbon emissions, and saving the environment; if you have children, spend a day totally devoted to playing with them – there is an aspect of this Goddess that I personally have only barely glimpsed that delights in the play of children

Contra-indications: littering, wasting energy or resources, squelching a child's happiness or creativity

May She be hailed!

Now Ostara was never a holiday that I particularly connected with, for all that I was born at the tail end of March, not too far past the Equinox. It was just not a time that I could ever get all that excited about. Maybe it's that I really dislike the mud and rain that so often comes with spring or perhaps that I know summer with its heat and bugs and nastiness is just around the corner, but while I do enjoy some elements of spring, Ostara just never excited me overmuch. I suppose I liked this season more as a child when I could indulge in egg hunts and Easter baskets. It wasn't really until I was an adult and had suffered the loss of a loved one that I came to appreciate Ostara's promise.

The funny thing about loss is how the truly traumatic ones come to define one's life. There's the 'before' and 'after' and in between is a chasm, a dividing line beyond which nothing is ever again the same as it was, or as one might hope. Every loss is a destruction, a decimation, a rending of the self. It weighs down the spirit. It hollows out the heart. It shatters one's sense of oneself in the world. What Eostre taught me is that every destruction like that is also a creation and holds within it the potential for rebirth. That sounds inconsequential and shallow, cliché even, but when all color, light, and joy has been stripped from your world with the death of a loved one (in my case, my adopted mom), it is no small thing at all. It is everything, the giving back of life-restoring breath, a resuscitation, a reanimation, a calling back to life. Sometimes, it's the only lifeline visible in the dark places into which the heart can sink.

In its essence, that is what this holy tide is: a calling back to life. It's a renewal not only of the land, but of the senses, heart, and spirit too. We are changed and crafted by the lives we live. Our experiences wear us down, hone us, and in the end, define who and what we are. I think perhaps grief does that most of all, though something of this process is inherent in all the struggles of living. Ostara promises renewal in the midst of those struggles. She holds out to us Her blessings, Her elixir of life, and love, and yes, even joy. She unerringly has the power to tease the heart into joy and that is precisely what this time, this holiday is about: a rebirth of joy.

Joy is not something we talk a lot about as Heathens. Our worship should be filled with joy. It should be filled with celebration. We never talk about that or emphasize it though, and sometimes it seems as though our very ritual structure is designed to downplay it. We're sadly Protestant in our expectations as contemporary Heathens. Yet Eostre stands in stark contrast to that grim uniformity. She brings the gift of celebration, of dance, of song, of graceful rejoicing, of gaiety. Most importantly of all She lifts the spirit gently up and out of the morass of pain that is so often a byproduct of living and loving.

Perhaps that is why the egg is such a potent symbol of Her power. It represents hope, as the rabbit represents growth. We can laugh at these symbols, find them cute, even silly and perhaps that is Her gift as well, for I believe that play was an important aspect of Her mysteries. We need to reclaim that. We need to be fearless in reclaiming that playfulness. Sometimes playfulness is precisely the tonic necessary to the grimness that life can so often deliver. If it takes a rabbit and some chocolate eggs to teach us how to do that, then so be it!

Eostre whispers Her promises at this time. She calls us to remember that it is not only grief that transforms the spirit but that great joy can do so as well. She calls us to a love affair with joy, and will teach us how to court it with ardor. She is all about the promise of life, for as much as life can entrench us in sadness and grief, it is also filled with beauty, wonder, courage, grace, magnificent opportunities for connection, and yes, even joy. There is joy in living. She will teach us to seek all of that out. She may even teach us to revel in it. Surely She will show us how to hold onto these things with zeal and zest and fervor, to see us through the darkest of times, to sustain our spirits, cushion our hearts, and to lead us to finding our own internal spring.

She is a Goddess of springtime after all, the dawn of the year that parallels the dawn of the heart after grief. Her grace is the easing of burdens, or the finding of a measure of happiness while in the midst of them. Hers is the gift of space and time and breath: a liminal moment stolen from between the dark force of Yule and the hot passions of Litha, a moment given to grace and play and to the quest for that restorative joy. She is a Goddess of growth and hope and tremendous courage to embrace living in all its permutations.

Ostara is about the future. It reminds us of the promise of things to come, of the turning of cycles, the shifting of seasons and the slow healing that time alone can bring. This time tells us that nothing is eternal. Nothing is unchanging. Nothing remains the same. It reminds us to hang on, hang in there, knowing that in time the cycle will turn again and we will find ourselves ready for the renewal that this time and this Goddess can so kindly bring. Moreover we are reminded not to scoff at such kindness for in the end, before anything else, She is the force that sustains.

In a way, one could say that Eostre really is the 'reason for the season.' She gave Her name not only to our Heathen and Pagan holiday of Ostara/Eostre, but also to the Christian celebration of Easter. This was one Goddess Who just would not go away! For all that, like with Hreðe, we really don't know all that much about Her. Bede wasn't terribly forthcoming in his *de Temporibus Ratione*, and aside from a minor notation in the *Heimskringla*, that's really the only source of information we have on this Goddess.

We do know that the name Ostara or Eostre means 'to shine,' and scholars of Proto-Indo-European studies connect Her to the Greek Eos and Sanskrit Ushas, both Goddesses of sunrise and the dawn. Scholar Rudolf Simek further suggests that She is a "spring-like fertility Goddess." Obviously Her primary symbols are the rabbit and the egg, indicative of fertility and potentiality. I'm making an intuitive leap here, but I'd also posit that given the delight children seem to take in Her holiday (or at least those folk customs that have come down to us), that She is a Goddess of young children, or childhood as well. As sunrise awakens the day, driving back the darkness of night, so She awakens the land from the dark slumber of winter. She is a Goddess of new beginnings, new life, the quickening of the land and by extension, of pregnancy and birth.

The egg, as Her symbol, is not only indicative of the potential for new life, but for hope as well and that is no small thing at all, especially in the uncertain times in which we live. Our ancestors' world was uncertain too, filled with the potential for far more physical peril than we, on a daily basis, face. But ours is not without its struggles, its fears, its tragedies and harm. We need our Deities of hope and hope is very much Eostre's gift.

She is also a Goddess of fertility, evidenced in part by the fact that the rabbit is Her symbol. Rabbits are powerful symbols of fertility and fecundity. I would encourage women who wish to conceive to make special offerings to Eostre at this time. She is a Goddess Who blesses childbirth. (The healing Goddess Hlif can also help in this). I would also encourage those mothers who have recently had children to make offerings of thanks, perhaps even asking Her protection on the newborns. Older children can be gifted with stuffed rabbits, blessed in Her name, or given rabbit charms blessed in Her name with the wish for health and protection. Eostre is about potential and progress, birth, growth, and regeneration. This is what captures Her attention; these are the realms in which She moves. Children, by their very nature, embody those things inherently; and I believe based on my own experience with Her that She is a tremendously kind Goddess Who would look on a mother's prayers for children or for her children with grace and benevolence.

In the end, this is yet another of our Deities that we shall really only know by virtue of our willingness to engage one on one with Them. We shall learn about Her through the act of honoring Her. Let's work together to deepen our knowledge and understanding of this very special Goddess. May She be hailed!

Prayer to Eostre

I praise Eostre, Goddess of the Dawn;
rising mighty in the east, You bless us.
I praise Eostre, Goddess of the fertile fields.
With victory and fruitful luck, You nourish us.

I praise Eostre, Goddess of new beginnings.
With strength and resilience, You fortify us.
Shine Your light upon us, Holy Goddess.
Make our words and deeds mighty in Your eyes.
Replenish us daily with Your light.
We hail You, Gracious Goddess of the dawn.
We hail You, Eostre, after Whom Spring itself is named.
Please, make us fruitful. Hail.

Prayer to the Goddess of Spring

We hail the Goddess of spring,
of vibrancy, of stirring bounty,
of the waking earth,
that readies itself for the seed.
We hail the Goddess of sunshine,
and cycles, and changes,
and all good and terrifying things.
We pray for fertility in our works,
of minds, and hearts, and hands.
We pray for blessings,
and the gift
of hope's manifestation.
We hail the Goddess of spring,
as Her bounty covers the land.
Eostre, be Thou praised.

Ways to Honor Ostara/Eostre

Colors: pastel colors, blues, pinks, yellows, oranges – colors of the dawn, and also those traditionally associated with Easter

Symbols and Altar suggestions: rabbits, eggs, spring flowers, seeds and seedlings, ferns, rich dark soil, images of pregnant women, of children and babies, vulva and phallic images

Food and Drink: milk, eggs, a German wine called 'Liebfraumilch,' chocolate, raspberries, fresh fruits and vegetables, nettles, damiana, angelica, mugwort, saffron (all fertility herbs)

Service offerings: spend a day running errands or cleaning house for a pregnant friend; plant a garden; give a child a gift; donate to an organization like Save the Children (www.savethechildren.org), the Coalition for Improving Maternity Services (www.mother friendly.org), the Women's Fund Network (www.fundforward.org), SHARE (www.nationalshare.org), or Breast Cancer Research Foundation (www.bcrfcure.org) in Her name.

Contraindications: doing anything to harm a child; not taking responsibility for one's children; neglecting to pay child support; doing things that show disrespect for or damage the land

WALPURGISNACHT

Another of the holy tides common to Heathens, Wiccans, and many Pagans is Walpurgis or Beltane. While the focus of the holiday might vary somewhat depending on which tradition one is coming from, the underlying theme remains the same: May 1 is a time to celebrate the blossoming of the land, of its vibrancy and fecundity and by extension it is a holiday that also celebrates our own vibrancy, fecundity, and sexuality.

Historically, this holiday celebrated the joy of having a fully stocked larder. The Anglo-Saxons called it *Thrimilci*, 'three-milk month' because this was a time when, after the cold, hard months of winter, the cows could be milked three times a day. There were, after months of winter rationing, eggs and milk aplenty. So many of our sacred tides involve food, or a celebration of food, of having enough to eat and to sustain ourselves and I find this very telling. Our ancestors didn't have Wal-Mart or Stop and Shop. They lived off the land and followed its cycles and if the crops failed, perhaps they starved. People were far more intimately connected to Erda, Mother Earth, than we are today. The average person knew that if Her favor was not forthcoming, that the coming winter might prove a very harsh one indeed.

While Spring Equinox celebrations honor the end of winter and the springtime awakening of the land, Beltane and Walpurgis specifically honor the plenty that comes from the land. Trees are blooming, flowers are bursting into a bright panoply of color, the first planting has probably already occurred, and of course, it's a time of 'spring fever.' Many of the traditional elements of this holiday emphasize sexuality, the stirring of the blood, the celebration of the flesh. We have the May-pole, which is, to quote the cult-classic *Wicker Man*, a phallic symbol. I think that perhaps because this holiday occurs not long after the first tilling of the soil that there is a natural connection between planting of crops with the planting of a different type of seed. That is why sex in all its various forms is such a common offering in private Beltane rites. It's a wonderful time for those who are connected to Deities strongly associated with sex, or who have a strong connection to the land to gift those Deities and land spirits with sexual energies...if possible, by having intercourse outside, on the grass and soil and consecrating the energy to Their use. (Of course it goes without saying that this should only be done on one's own private land with consenting adults. It is not necessary to do this in order to honor this holiday, but it is one way for couples to celebrate together. For those not so inclined, this is a good time to honor Deities of love, romance, and sex and to honor those relationships that are most important in one's life be they romantic or not.).

Walpurgis has another, more arcane aspect to it as well. It is traditionally a holiday associated with magic, witchcraft, and the renewal of power. In the Northern Tradition both the Goddess Freya and the Goddess Holda are strongly connected to this particular time. Both are Goddesses of witchcraft and occult power. Traditionally celebrated not on May 1, but on April 30, Walpurgis was considered a time of immense occult power. Just as fecundity is returning to the land, so it is returning to the unseen rivers and streams of energy from which magicians might pull their power.

I often suggest, for those planning a Beltane ritual, that they plan a rite that honors the Vanir Gods and Goddesses. This family of Deities was strongly associated with abundance, fertility, sexuality, and wealth in all its forms. It is also a time to honor Earth, and the sacred element of Fire. Fire holds a very important role in Norse cosmology: it is our eldest ancestor, being along with ice, the element from which all life sprung. Fire is very important on so many levels both ritually and in our everyday life. For our ancestors it was an immense gift: with the blessings of fire, one could cook one's food, warm one's home, drive off animals in the night. One could temper metal, work glass, craft clay into usable items, forge not only weapons but things that made life better for one's tribe and community. Fire is intimately bound up with civilization. For all its wildness and destructive power, fire is essential to human creativity.

One traditional accoutrement to any good Beltane ritual (provided it can be held outdoors) is a bonfire. Fire is intimately bound up in the celebrations of this Holy Tide because fire is not only essential to civilized life, but symbolically represents vitality, life, lust, and passion. So Beltane is a good time to honor Deities of Fire as well as Deities of abundance and sexuality. It is a good to time laugh, rejoice, pour out offerings and say 'thank you' for all the blessings we have been given throughout the year. Honor the spirits of fire, who, by their very presence, hallow and transform. Celebrate the abundance that we have been given. I often honor the Goddess Gefion, who is associated with both wealth and land at this time. Regardless of which Deities you decide to honor: rejoice. That is what this holiday is all about in a way: honoring the sacred spark of life and its continuation and transformation.

It seems odd to me to be sitting at my computer on a dismal, rainy, dreary April day, with the chill in the air serving as a palpable reminder that spring isn't quite here yet and writing about Beltane. Beltane is supposed to be about celebration, passion, fertility, prosperity, magic, heat, and yes, sex. Yep. Beltane is about sex (at least in part) and on days like today, that type of joyous celebration seems very far away. Still, if you'll pardon the inevitable pun, Beltane is coming and like any of our other holy tides, it deserves a bit of thought.

I've been dreading writing this particular column for the past week or so, ever since I realized that Beltane and Walpurgis were right around the corner. This is the tail end of the school year for me (I'm in graduate school) and papers are due, exams must be prepared for, then of course there are all the professional writing deadlines that are piling up. Thinking about what I've always considered a rather 'happy-go-lucky' holiday was not on my personal agenda of things I wanted to be doing (or had the time to do). Still, even for me, misanthropic and overworked though I sometimes may be, it's difficult not to get pulled into the energetic momentum of this time. With Beltane after all, we lay to rest, once and for all, the inertia of the preceding winter. What began with the land's seemingly lazy resistance to the inevitable pull of spring bursts full force into bloom with the turning of the seasonal wheel to May.

At its core, Beltane is about planting. At Ostara we honored the readiness of the land to receive the seed; at Beltane we actually plant those seeds, be they literal or metaphorical. At Ostara we celebrated the potential fertility of the land; at Beltane we revel in its actuality. This is kind of where the sex part of things comes in. Beltane is about life, growth, and all the messiness of unrestrained passion. It's about the joining of seed to soil, body to body, physicality to physicality, and the potential joining of sperm to egg. It's about bringing forth new life, new possibilities, new reasons to celebrate one's traditions. This is a time when the land, at least for us Northern Tradition folks, was traditionally blessed by happy couples having sex in fields, on the soil where their fluids and carnal enjoyment of each other only served to feed the land itself and further ensure its blossom. The May pole, a symbol we all know and love, is (as any fan of the original *Wicker Man* knows) "a phallic symbol." The magic of Beltane is held forth in the erect penis and spurting seed, and in our bodies' ability to experience pleasure. This, more than any other holy tide reminds us that living is cause for celebration. There is pleasure in being alive, pleasure that, at the appropriate times, can and should be indulged.

Far more than being about the celebrating the penis (or the vulva, or any other body part – not that there's anything wrong with that; celebrate away, folks), I would interpret the wisdom and 'medicine' of this holiday on a broader level. I believe Beltane

159

reminds us that our bodies are sacred. In the Northern Tradition the physical container of the soul is so valued that it's actually considered part of the soul matrix. That's right: each physical vessel of incarnation is intimately connected to one's soul, an integral part of it. We're incarnate for a reason. Our bodies are the tools and conduits by and through which we experience everything, including the Divine. Moreover, they may even be the way the Gods experience us – spirituality being, like so many things, a two way street. Far from needing to escape from the flesh, Beltane reminds us that there's an awful lot of wisdom inherent in being *in* the flesh too.

One of the Goddesses commonly honored within the Northern Tradition at this time is the Goddess Freya. She is a tremendously powerful Goddess, associated with sexuality, eroticism, passion, battle and war, fierce fighting, cunning strategy, prosperity and wealth, physical beauty, and witchcraft and sorcery. One of Her primary and most important lessons is about knowing one's own worth (and being unwilling to compromise that in any way). That can be a hard, hard lesson for many people today (especially, I hate to say it, for women). Freya's lessons often involve self-satisfaction and confidence in one's physical being (and I'm not talking just about sexuality here). This is a Goddess who knows how to celebrate the flesh, both its passion and its power. Here is a Goddess not afraid to take up space, claim Her territory, defend Her territory, and own Her strength. Here is a Goddess who can teach Her devotees to say "where I stand is holy ground" and mean it.

Beltane's call is a call to that type of commitment and courage. It reminds us that our physicality is sacred, no matter what messages we may imbibe from our families, our culture, the media. We're called to stand up and live our truth. Learning to express ourselves well physically and kinetically, learning to have both trust and confidence in our bodies is part of honoring this tremendous gift that we've been given. It's part of living our truth. Tending to our bodies, just as we tend to the land is good and sacred work. Our bodies support and nourish us just as the land supports and nourishes us. One might see in the microcosm of one, the macrocosm of the other. Sometimes that is the way these things work. So learning to nourish, care for, protect and defend one's physical form and knowing to the marrow of one's being that this might even be a sacred *obligation*, is all part of what Beltane can teach us. Imagine how our lives would be different if treating our bodies kindly, loving our flesh, and living healthily was something we could all do with joy. How many of us can stand naked in front of the mirror and say, "I love my physical form" and really mean it? Freya can teach us how, if we honor Her rightly and well. Beltane's wisdom can show us the way.

Our world is out of balance. I think that it is inevitable that our collective psyches bear the brunt of that sickness. We have come to embody it physically. Our bodies and the way we relate to them have suffered generations of fear, shame, and abuse because we have forgotten that simple truth that flesh is sacred. We have forgotten so much in abandoning our ancestral ways and our Holy Powers but most of all, we've forgotten how to interact with ourselves in a healthy manner. We've forgotten how to love being. Beltane calls us to throw ourselves into the inevitable change this time brings, the momentum, the urgency, the growing sense of joy and movement that fills the land. It urges us to seek our passions, to find that which nourishes us and to live it fully each and every day of our lives. Beltane's wisdom is, above all else, a call to embodied joy.

Moreover, Beltane reminds us not just to honor our physical bodies, but to rejoice in the physical experience of the natural world. That world is a gift in all its beautiful, breathtaking, sometimes confusing diversity. This holy tide calls us to move beyond our dearly held paradigms into the reality of being: beyond our dichotomies (sexual, gender and otherwise) into the rich tapestry of possibility inherent in creation. Diversity is nature's greatest achievement. As we celebrate the beauty, bounty, and blessings of corporeality, physicality, and incarnation, we're reminded to celebrate it *all*, not just those forms which are comfortable. Nature is an explosion of diversity and this is a lesson we can take to heart as we honor our bodies: we're part of that diversity too. As a good friend of mine once pointed out: there is no 'normal.' Let's do away with the idea of 'normal.' There is only what is normal for us, for each individual, one by one. Beltane gives us a chance to celebrate that and given how much hate is in our world for any type of diversity of being, that too, is no small thing.

This is a holy tide all about action and restoration. We have the chance as we move into May to recommit to picking up those threads of connection – to our Gods, our ancestors, the land itself, and to ourselves – sundered so long ago. Healing that damage doesn't happen with grand gestures; it happens with small commitments, like planting a seed. That's Beltane's wisdom. It's about making those promises, to ourselves, our families, our communities that we will see fulfilled with the coming harvest. It's about deciding what we wish to harvest in the coming season for ourselves, our lives and our spirituality. It's about deciding what kind of person we would like to be when the harvest is done.

Beltane is coming. Emphasis on the coming, folks. Beltane, or Walpurgis if you prefer, is right around the corner. This is the time to whip it out, love your bits, and tap whatever and whomever you have in your life to tap. And do it with joy and celebration while you're at it too. Fuck fiercely, my friends, and call on the Gods and Goddesses of sex, love, eroticism, sensuality, and pleasure when you do it. Those Deities, by the way, are also Deities of abundance and wealth. Think there might be a connection?

Beltane is about sex. Well, okay, it's not just about sex but it is about loosing creativity and readying the land for summer growth, and the explosion of life that comes with the turning of the seasonal year to spring. It's a seasonal festival all about fertility and fire, abundance, and rampant, unadulterated, unapologetic creativity. It's about coming and the burning in the loins, and the earth's seasonal orgasm that brings a flood of life into being as spring turns to summer and the land yields its bounty to the blazing beauty of the sun. In our parlance, simple creatures that we are, it's about fucking.

I used to poo-poo those who worked primarily with sexual energies. I really did. It's so terribly easy to get distracted by pleasure, to allow it to pull one from one's purpose rather than to harvest and channel those energies toward furthering one's ritual and magical goals. I suppose with anything one must be careful, but pleasure – specifically sexual pleasure – seemed particularly prone to pulling people away from devotion to the Gods. It's true, pleasure doesn't have the raw, brutal frankness that pain can bring, but it does raise a shit-ton of energy; and it's fun, and just as the darker, more brutal energies are important, so too is it important to embrace the energies of lust and life and love. Why? Because we live in a fucked up world, that's why. We live in a fuck-phobic world. We live in a culture so infiltrated, permeated, contaminated by prurient, anti-sex, fundamentalist (monotheistic) attitudes that it's no wonder we're ready to kill each other and do so every day. (Just turn on the news.)

Our culture is amazingly anti-sex. I'll go ya one further. Heathenry is amazingly anti-sex, or rather it's anti-interesting (non-vanilla) sex. I was, for instance, once all but forced out of a group not because of anything that I myself had done (although plenty of people objected to my approach and praxis), but specifically because of my *friendship* with a noted BDSM activist and educator. I routinely get harassed partly because I do ordeal work, but over and above that (and I'll admit to the non ordeal worker, ordeal can be discomfiting in and of itself) because my detractors automatically (and inaccurately) twin ordeal with BDSM and kink. Plus we talk about it, and unapologetically too. We don't shroud it in a veil of secrecy and shame, as though it's something dirty. I suppose it's okay for Heathens to have sex, but let's not actually enjoy it or bring the sacred into it. This is what happens when you draw your dominant demographic from white Protestant fundamentalism and never really do anything about that monotheistic influenced mental filter. You bring these same ridiculous attitudes right on into your new religion.

Then, I see people who are never touched. I'm not talking sex, I'm talking simple physical contact. I see people every day who haven't been hugged in a decade. I see people who are starving physically and emotionally for basic human contact. There have been scientific studies done proving that if infants are denied human affection – skin to skin affection – they can die. Why should it be any different for adults? Even if they don't die in body, they can wither away inside in their hearts and minds and spirits. Moreover, I see people who have never touched themselves and now I am talking sex and I think it a moral crime to fill someone with guilt and shame for the pleasure their own body can give them. We should love our bodies. We have to live here after all. Let's take some pleasure in that…in our own bodies and those of our partners' too.

Bits are great: lady bits, man bits, trans bits, in between bits, intersex bits, all variations of bits – and by bits, in case you haven't figured it out, I mean genitals. It's one of the things that mother Nature got fabulously right. And you know what? Let me self-disclose in the spirit of Beltane. I particularly love cock. Bring on the Maypole, baby. Let's just get that out of the way right now. I love the man bits especially. I love the fact that our bodies are capable of so much pleasure and I especially love how the power sexual activity raises can be used for our own health (I've a Tantrika friend who swears that an orgasm a day keeps miasma and sickness away) but also to challenge the dominant social paradigm. Sex magic, bitches. We has it.

I talk a lot about fighting the dominant, monotheistic filter, the lens through which we view the world, inculcated in us with the rise of monotheism, driven by the doctrine of discovery, and virulently protective of its hegemony. I believe there is a sentience there. I believe it to be malevolent to all creativity, spirituality, and life. I fight that filter with every ounce of my being, every day, with every bit of work that I do. Often it fights back. Those of you who've walked this road know what I'm talking about. Those of you who haven't seen it yet, haven't really come face to face with it in any conscious way, take heart, you can still fight it and some of that fighting can be done on your back (or your hands and knees, or quite a few other tasty positions).

You see, the filter isn't subtle. If one engages long enough in this fight, if one looks long enough at the field of battle it becomes readily apparent what some of our strongest tools with which to drive it back and break its hold on our world might be. It's told us time and time again throughout generations. You want to know the weapons to use to fight it? Look at what it proscribes. Look at what it condemns. Look at what it tells us not to do. (You think sex doesn't top that list? We have a nation permeated with monotheistic values and a world where 80% of the wealth lies with 20% of the people – and those numbers are a decade old, it's probably more imbalanced by now – and yet our politicians are bitching about abortion, birth control, gay marriage, and sex. Because you know, consenting adults having sex is more of a threat to our personhood, future, and nationhood than starving children and world peace.) The filter tells us precisely how to fight it. All we have to do is pay attention.

So here's my little plan to fuck the filter right in its face. Here's a little something almost everyone can do, and some of it is even fun.

Step one: honor your ancestors. One of the first practices condemned when monotheism became the law of the land was that of making regular offerings to the dead. The spirits of our ancestors are our protection. They are our strength. They sustain and protect us and they are a wall of power and sense through which the filter has no purchase.

Step two: honor the Gods and Goddesses of your people, of your heart, of your land. Celebrate a multitude of Deities. Pour out offerings to Them, pray, honor Them in any way you can.

Step three: fuck like there's no tomorrow.

Yeah, you read that right. Enjoy yourselves. Feel. Allow yourselves to get into the guts of the experience and feel. Don't stay numb. Don't pretend. Don't settle for mediocrity – especially not in bed. Get down (go down) and enjoy yourselves. Suck the ....um....marrow out of life, and by doing so, celebrate it. If you don't have a partner, or don't want one, don't despair. You have your fingers. You have toys, lots of toys. You can still have a steaming good time and you can still work some powerful magic. For those a little more adventurous (and a little more skilled in the ins and outs of magic), you can take the energy raised during sex and channel it to a specific purpose. This is sex magic.

Sex magic is a powerful tool in the fight against the filter and there's no better time to get your 'feet,' yeah 'feet,' wet than at Beltane. Tap into the currents of erotic energies that the land itself is unleashing at this time. When you're having sex, feel the energy flowing around you and through you. Feel the energy building as you near orgasm. If you're bold and really want to work it, bring yourself right to the edge of orgasm but don't allow yourself to tumble over that boundary. Do that again and again and finally, when you're ready, when you feel like you've taken all you can there, allow yourself orgasm and focus that release into whatever working you wish. If you and your partner can climax at the same time, that's ideal but not necessary for this to be an effective means of magic.

The secret, by the way, to making the best use of every drop of power spilled, is to create the energetic and mental framework, the focus of the spell before you ever touch yourself or your partner. Have it laid out and set well in advance. If you work with sigils, have your sigil ready to go. Do not wait until the moment of orgasm to decide where you're sending the energy. You will be fucked. Literally and magically. All that good, sweet, energy will be wasted. It also works best if one partner is the power generator and the other the technician who focuses the power raised. Most relationships have their power dynamics whether the couple admits it or not. Admit it, acknowledge it, figure it the fuck out before you...you know, fuck for world peace, and get on with it.

For those wanting to do some off the charts sex magic, Beltane is the perfect time to do so. Want to celebrate the way some of your ancestors might have? Well, have a couple, as part of the ritual process, go off and have sex, channeling all the energy raised to a previously agreed-upon group goal. Have them perform what is euphemistically called the 'hieros gamos,' the sacred marriage. The couple chosen become embodiments of the dual energies of kundalini, the cosmic exhalation and inhalation, the thrust and moan, the push and pull, that form the pulsing heartbeat of the land itself at this time. Want to get fancy? Have more than one couple doing this at the same time. If you want to get really old school, do this out on the dirt, in your garden, in your fields, and feed the energy into the land. Have everyone else, while you've got your sacred couple doing this rite, go off and masturbate, right up to the edge but without tumbling over into orgasm. then have them go and work in the garden, work in the land, work in the dirt, feeding the energy that would have culminated into orgasm, into the rich lushness of the land, that the land instead might be readied, wet, and fertile. There are dozens of ways to do this type of working. If you have no goal in mind, feed that energy consciously in offering to one of your Deities. I've never found Freya, for instance, to object to a gift of pleasure. Energy is Energy. Power is Power. And sex holds within it the power of transformation and creation and that is no small thing with which to work.

So bring on the lube. Bring out the whips and chains. Bring out whatever gets you hot. If vanilla sex is where you're at: great. Have lots of it. If you're kinkier than fuck, get down with your bad self and enjoy. So long as everyone's of age and everyone's consenting, have at it. Most of all enjoy it.

My advice for Beltane? Go off and have a fine fucking day. And I mean that. Literally.

Because sex is fucking sacred. It's *all* sacred and it's about time we remembered that.

Happy Beltane.

LITHA/SUMMER SOLSTICE

Here is a solstice meditation for you, something simple that you can do as you end your day. Sit down in your sacred place, be it before a personal altar, before an ancestral altar, outside in a place of peace and quiet, in a bedroom...wherever. Sit down and light a candle and give thanks for fire. Give thanks for the warmth of the sun, for the heat of our bodies, for the fires of life, of passion, of inspiration. Give thanks to the spirits of fire that enabled our ancestors to cook their food, temper metal, blow glass and establish civilization. Give thanks for fire and for all good things.

Then think for a few moments on your year, that precious and fleeting span of time from Solstice to Solstice. Where were you last Litha? What were you doing? Who were you with? How has your life changed? What have you sacrificed and in what ways have you been blessed? Isn't it funny how the two so often go hand in hand?

Think on the past year and count its blessings, let the fabric of memory pass through your mental fingers as you contemplate its warp and weft. Then give thanks. We cannot know where we are going if we do not acknowledge where we came from. Give thanks to the fire that transforms all things. Give thanks to the ancestors that walk with us down roads both joyful and sometimes bleak. Give thanks and then breathe. Spend a few moments focusing on the rhythm of your breath, the inhalation as you take in life-giving air, the exhalation. This is what connects you to life. Our first act upon coming into the world is to inhale, our last act upon leaving it to exhale. Breathe and turn your attention to the coming year.

In the span of time between one Litha and the next, between the end of one holy fire and the kindling of the next, what are your goals and dreams? What do you want to accomplish? Where do you want to be when you stand and call to the Gods on the longest day of next year? What gifts would you seek? What legacy would you seek to craft? You are each ancestors in the making. The coming months are precious bricks in the foundation that you are crafting for those who come after you. What do you wish to craft this year? Think on that and perhaps ask the ancestors and Gods for their/Their blessings.

Breathe and ground. With each exhalation let the tension and stress, the roiling thoughts, the excess energies of your body sink into the earth. Feel yourself bound to it, like a tree tied to the soil by a thick network of roots, roots that enable one to be strong and supple. You may blow out the candle if you must leave your space, or if you will be there for a time, allow it to burn. Give thanks, always, give thanks, and praise the fire of the Solstice.

MABON

I adore this time of year. There's a crispness in the air, the herald of colder, darker things to come. The leaves are just beginning to change into what, in my region of the U.S., will soon become a riotous panoply of color. I live in the belly of the mountains, in the Hudson River Valley and fall is something to be celebrated here for its beauty alone. It's as if the lines of varied color show, for a few brief weeks, the very and varied musculature of the mountains, rippling, stretching and preparing for the long sleep of winter. It's an awe-inspiring sight.

Of course I would celebrate autumn anyway. I've never been a summer person and I greet the cooling days with immense joy. They bring me vitality, a renewed sense of purpose, and the feeling of an immense burden being lifted (i.e., the paralyzing heat of the summer!). Fall provides a feast for the senses: the smell of burning leaves, the sweet chill of cooling nights, the spice of Thanksgiving-time sweets, the rich tapestry of color inherent in the trees and harvest vegetables, and above all the transformation of nature's green into the reds, golds, oranges, siennas, and browns of autumn. What a glorious relief! What a joyous sight! Moreover, these seasonal changes remind me that we're rapidly passing out of the time of Harvest and moving instead into the time of internal reflection and quiet that can, ideally, be part of winter. That is no small thing to honor.

With the feast of Mabon, the Fall Equinox, we acknowledge the balance of light and dark, life and death, growth and rot. We honor all those things that enable our world to grow and restore itself. On this holy tide, we hail the hunter and the hunted, the predator and the prey, the plough and the scythe, the blessings of growth and of decay. We honor our resources, and the frugality and careful planning of every ancestor whose careful household management got their families safely through the cold constraints of winter. Mabon is a time of remembrance and of culling away, of honoring what we have, what we need, but also what we can provide to others. It is a time to look clearly at where we are weak in spirit, where we are strong, and where we stand somewhere in between, a time to take stock of our portion of gratitude and blessings for the coming season.

This is the season of the Hunter, who takes the old, the weak, the infirm. It is a season preceding those dark nights before Yule when the Wild Hunt is said to ride. It reminds us that the holy walks hand in hand with terror. The message of Mabon, when the land begins to wither, to hoard its resources, to slow the rhythms of its growth down, is that we too must, at some point in our lives, slow down, cast off those things that are brittle, withered, and weary. We too must look within, because for us also, physically, spiritually, emotionally there are cycles that we have no choice but to obey and within those cycles may lie both terror and beauty, gain and loss. Within those cycles, we prepare ourselves for both the holy and the terror that lies within.

Contemplation on the rhythms of the seasons, the turning of summer into fall, shows us that just as the earth has its temporary fallow periods, so too we may sometimes enter into periods where our faith seems to lie fallow. But if we do the necessary work, if we engage mindfully in right action, if we do not let loss and pain, or joy and celebration pull us too far astray, if we work hard to maintain − to the best of our ability − right relationships with ourselves, our ancestors, the Holy Powers, and the world at large, such fallowness can blossom into a rich and worthy harvest.

Tilling the hard and rocky soil of one's own soul, ploughing deep furrows into which one can plant the seeds of faith, nurturing that faith, waiting out those painful fallow periods for those carefully planted seeds to grow is the hardest thing we will ever do. So many of us have been taught that faith is its own self-contained sphere, that it is for Sundays, or ritual days, or those times when we specifically set out to say a prayer and make an offering, that anything else is for mystics and those not really connected to the regular, mundane world. In reality, faith is very much an everyday thing. It's an awareness, a way of being in the world, of relating to the Holy Powers (Gods, ancestors, vaettir all), our friends and families in a very specific and very mindful way. It's the lens through which we interact with the world and most of all with ourselves and everything that we are striving to create and build for ourselves and our future. Sometimes we have to work very hard to keep that lens in focus because faith isn't just for the occasional ritual, or holy tide; it's an every day, every moment thing even in the midst of the most tumultuous change or wrenching emotions. Life is challenging after all, and faith all the more so.

One of the most painful but also the most necessary ways of keeping faith vital, vibrant, and strong is going into our own darkness, dancing with our own shadow, fighting with our own demons. Through the blessings of the Hunter and His prey, we are invited to engage in the powerful process of self-evaluation and exploration. We are offered a key, a way to walk through that most terrifying of doorways. We are offered a knife, a cleansing, flensing blade whereby we may look within and slowly, painfully cut away those brittle masks, external distractions, and false sentimentalities that prevent us from engaging in any truly meaningful way not only with our Gods but with ourselves and each other as well. We are offered a chance to put aside the self-absorption and pride that so often keeps us from developing as whole beings. We must be for ourselves both predator and prey. We are charged to seek these things out within the complex labyrinths of our souls so that there will be room for the grace of awareness to flow. This is the sacred Hunt with which we can all engage.

What are the skills necessary to a good Hunter? The hunt demands patience, keen vision, and solitude. So too, does faith, at least sometimes. It demands efficient preparation and skill hard won through much practice. So too, does faith. In the end, a good hunter brings his or her bounty back to share with community and kin. That's what faith is about too. Let the good Hunter be our model as the wyrd of our lives unfolds before us. Let His skills become ours.

What about the prey? Efficient prey is fleet of foot, it knows it must traverse dangerous ground swiftly and well to sustain its life. It knows it cannot stop until, or if, by the power of the predator it is brought down. Then, and only then, does it yield and cease its flight. So too must we seek out the integrity of our souls with the fierce survival instinct of an animal engaged in this primal dance. So too should we yield ourselves only to the final blow of our own divinely inspired hunt for from that submission, the grace of spiritual power grows.

Mabon marks a time of transition. The potential hunger of winter lurks just around the corner, if we are not careful, if we are not lucky, if we do not do the necessary work. The grace inherent in the harvest is that we're given the opportunity to evaluate and prepare for that hunger, and the same holds true for the hungers of our hearts and souls. Hail to the Hunter and Hail to the Prey. Hail to the terror and hail to the season's rejoicing. Hail to the coming darkness of Winter: the winter without, and all the little winters within, because Mabon tells us that from the darkness new blessings can flow.

WINTER NIGHTS

October is the month of Samhain, the month in which some of us celebrate Winter Nights, the month immediately preceding the Day of the Dead, the month which is, in so much of Paganism, given over to honoring the ancestors. I think this is good. Granted, I think it is even better to honor the ancestors consistently throughout the year but I am glad we have a holy tide centering around celebrating those who came before us. It's all too easy to forget about them in a world constantly obsessed with the young, the new, the up and coming.

So I want to suggest a challenge. The goal of this challenge is to give people the opportunity to consciously deepen their own ancestral practices. That connection is important. There is a Lukumi proverb that says, "We stand on the shoulders of our dead," because, as another proverb states, "The knife cannot carve its own handle." We are part of a line of men and women, connected to us by blood, or perhaps only by heart and spirit (for spiritual ancestors are as important as our physical ones) stretching back to the beginning of our world. That is a tremendous amount of strength, wisdom, and luck supporting us, a tremendous reservoir of power upon which we can draw; because our ancestors want us to succeed, to be happy, whole, successful beings. They're in our corner, so to speak.

The only thing they ask in return is recognition. Those that were part of our family line remain part of our family line, corporeality notwithstanding. Learning to properly and consistently honor them is a very important piece in the puzzle of one's spirituality. It's foundational. One doesn't have to know the names of one's ancestors to honor them. They know us, because they are connected to us by an unbreakable bond. It's only necessary to call them, collectively if that is the absolute best one can do. Beyond a certain point, we must all issue that collective call because I doubt any of us can trace our ancestral lines back to pre-history! Those that are adopted have four lines – maternal, paternal, adopted maternal, adopted paternal – upon which they can call, not to mention most of us have spiritual kin, those people who have guided and mentored, supported, and taught us but who are not related to us by blood. They're ancestors of a type too.

If one's immediate family was malicious or hurtful, they need not be honored. Go further back. For everyone, there is a point in one's line where the dead will be supportive. You might have to reach far, far back, generations upon generations, but it's worth doing. Nor does honoring one's dead take a tremendous amount of effort. I always recommend setting up and maintaining an ancestral shrine: a table or shelf that is given over only to them. I admit, that living as I do in a spacious home, that for some this might be a luxury. As nice as it is to have an ancestor altar, it's not absolutely necessary. Those for whom this is an impossibility can still honor their dead. The act of honoring comes from the mind and heart after all; what we do physically is an external outgrowth of that mindfulness. The ways in which we can honor our dead are endless.

With that in mind, my challenge for October is this: each and every day of this month, do something to honor your ancestors. It doesn't matter what it is, but celebrate them. Instead of just giving them one ritual at the end of October, give them every day of the entire month. Talk about them. Share their stories. Give them offerings. Do things in their honor. Put up their pictures. Maybe, if you can, set up an altar. Visit graves and make sure they're clean and maybe bring flowers, maybe share a meal with your dead. I'm sure that you can come up with ideas for celebrating your dead that I haven't even considered. But honor them – commit an entire month, thirty one days, to living in mindful, ongoing partnership with your dead. One day, whether we have choose to have children or not, we will be ancestors. Let's do for them now, what we might wish done for us: let us keep them in living memory, in celebration and honor.

Hail to the dead,
and to the Gods who guard them.
Hail to those who have come before us.
Hail to those who stand behind us.
Hail to those upon whose strength and sacrifices,
successes and failures we feed.
Hail to our ancestors.
Hail them.

Samhain heralds in the season of grace. As the earth grows colder, entering into its dying time, turning within, we too are given the opportunity to look within. We're given the chance to attend to ourselves and to the dusty, unexamined parts of our lives. Samhain heralds in a terrifying season where we are asked to radically embrace loss, to willingly and moreover actively journey within, into the labyrinthine passages of our hearts and minds and souls; we're asked to journey into memory and to sweep out those hidden internal corners all those things that no longer serve us, our Gods, our spirituality, or our lives at large. Here, we're given a chance to take stock and to reevaluate. We're challenged to remember our successes but more importantly, our losses, our failures, those moments of grief and shame. These things too are building blocks and guides, sometimes much more powerful ones than those crafted from more pleasant experiences. More importantly, we're asked to rejoice, to give thanks for the blessings that have fallen, often unexpectedly, into our hands throughout the previous months.

Samhain is about the memory of things long past and long gone. Loss has value. Loss teaches us what we have. It teaches us how to recognize and treasure the smallest of blessings in our lives. It brings perspective. It hones and makes our measure. Samhain is a time when, above all else, we are asked to honor loss.

The dead walk with us now. They always do, watching over and guiding us, suffering as we suffer, celebrating as we rejoice. While our ancestors are always with us there's something special about this time. Perhaps it's only that we are primed to be more open to their presence around Samhain, perhaps it is that with the world withering in beauty all around us, it is easier to put ourselves in a place where we can consciously touch them. Let us remember them now: their names, their stories, their struggles, their sacrifices. Let us carry their graves on our backs, in our hearts, in our minds, in our memories. We are here because of them. We are their legacy: generation after generation of human brutality, suffering, indifference, and loss and we are here. Generation after generation of human celebration, courage, integrity, and hope and we are here. Let us praise them. Let us remember their names. Let us eat of their stories. Let us imbibe their sorrows and their joys. We are their living trust.

In this we are connected to the flow of experience greater and older and bigger than we shall ever be. In this we stand as one with our dead, one with their strength, wisdom, and the flow of experience. In this we take our place in a line of blood, bone, sinew, and power stretching back to the beginning of time. In this they live again and their sufferings have the power to transform our world, our lives, our culture, our time. Give them that voice. At Samhain we are reminded that to neglect our honoring of the dead is to stifle their voices, smother their stories, invalidate the tangled tapestries of their lives. It is to commit a crime against memory, piety, and honor. We are called upon to celebrate them always but on this single night of all the year let us lay ourselves down on the body of the earth and pour our tears out in offering: the greatest wealth to be found in the land of the dead after remembrance. Wyrd forgets nothing. Let us bless that remembrance with our own.

Samhain is a season of terror, of loss, of painful gratitude but also of potential renewal and reawakening. We carry the hopes of all our long line of dead into our own futures, futures that we have the power and potential to craft and weave each moment of every day. That is the final grace of this season: a call to action, to mindful reverence, to living awake, aware, and connected to all that was and all that we have the potential to be.

So give thanks, above all else, on Samhain night give thanks. It is a small thing but sometimes the smallest of gifts is enough.

YULE

Yule is one of my favorite holidays. Perhaps this is simply because it's so commonly associated with Odin and the Wild Hunt within Heathenry and I love Odin dearly. Perhaps it is because I treasure the dark time of winter, the emotions evoked by the decorations and festivities of this time, and the sense of solitude that for me, comes with the shortening of the days. Perhaps it's a combination of the two. I don't know. For whatever reason, however, I gravitate toward those holy tides that fall in the dark time of our seasonal cycle, those that grace the months between the last vestiges of summer and the first true bleakness of winter. I find that this time has the power to both cleanse and nourish like no other time of the year can.

This is not all together a comfortable process. Indeed the final few weeks before the Solstice are, for me, a time of almost brutal interiority. There is something about those interstitial nights between the coming of Yule and the actual New Year that send me hurtling inward on a journey of paring down, paring away, and yes, even personal mourning – all this in the midst of external celebration. It is a sometimes puzzling paradox because Yule is a powerful time, for all that it is adorned with rituals of celebration and sharing; it is, at its heart, a time to seek both the darkness and the light alone.

For Yule we wait in darkness. We wait for the turning of the seasonal cycles, the procession of Sunna's march across the sky, the driving back ever so slowly of the darkness of winter and we wait the return of the blessing of light. In the stillness of midwinter, we face a seasonal reminder of our ending; we celebrate our mortality in miniature, the microcosm of that final journey as our world spins inevitably first into darkness and then again into warmth and light. That darkness beckons us and it is a season of deepest mystery.

The mystery of the Yule season lies in its complement of bounty and terror. Darkness governs this time complete with an ingrained longing for light. We adorn our homes with evergreens and the evergreens with tiny lights. We light candles and seek the warmth of family and fellowship and this is one of the blessings of this holy tide, that it summons forth charity and a desire for celebration, for the warmth of friends and loved ones. Yule reminds us that once our ancestors would have huddled around a burning Yule log in their long houses, or a hearth fire in their huts. They would have huddled in forced companionship driven together by the unyielding necessity of escaping the winter's cold and sharing the resources of tribe, village, and kin through the barren time when the fields lay fallow. Our world is different. We now have the luxury of seeking togetherness out or avoiding it at our whim. Yet the darkness outside the window at Yule, when the days are the shortest they will ever be, reminds us that even in the midst of plenty, we are alone. Even in the midst of celebration, we are part of that darkness too.

Yule is about the endless dance of opposites locked in their taut embrace. It is about the cosmic dance of light and darkness, Muspelheim and Niflheim, synergy and stillness, expansion and contraction, life and death all at once. The darkness holds those things up to us and we seek the light in terror.

Darkness can be a powerful teacher. It surrounds us from without; it burbles up from within reminding us of all we have lost, all we might lack, all those to whom we are 'Other.' Yule is the holy time of that sacred Other − whatever that may be. We've lost the ability to frame this journey in any sacred context so instead, our loneliness, our aloneness may strike us especially hard at this time. We may become that 'Other' even to ourselves. This is a blessing, a terrible, difficult, ultimately magnificent blessing, for Yule brings with its mysteries a wonderful opportunity to open ourselves up, to lay ourselves down in joyful humility and gratitude, grace, and longing before that which is rendered Holy by this dance. We are given the chance to acknowledge that we ride within cycles ever so much greater than ourselves. Yule is about what we do with that dance of opposites within ourselves, how we make a tenuous, ever-shifting peace with it – or not – and what we allow to bloom from that; for it is in the midst of that darkness that our souls and hearts and minds are made fertile soil for the grace of the Gods to flourish.

Mystics have known this all along. Across traditions, across time, across cultures there is a common thread binding those who seek the Gods in this way: an acknowledgement of the power of that spiritual darkness to enmesh, ensnare, and ultimately to drag one down into the embrace of the Holy. It is the blessing of barrenness hiding behind the festivities of Yule-time's public face; and each winter we are given a powerful chance to court that barrenness for ourselves, to go within and see what really lies behind the masks we so deftly wear for others and for ourselves too.

The Wild Hunt is said to ride at this time, dead men all, including the God who leads them. They shriek across the chill and stormy skies seeking out any who stray hapless into their path. Humility might save a person caught unawares, when the Hunt comes thundering down; the humility to bow ones head and recognize, as we so often fail to do in our frenetic and unbalanced world, that we stand shaking in the presence of the Holy. We structure our rituals carefully, and call our Gods with equal care, standing safe in the embrace of civilization and community consensus. It's times like this though, when the Hunt rides mad and hungry through the darkness, casting ravenous spears into the flesh of our unconscious that we're reminded how fragile and paper-frail our illusions of safety really are. The tales of the Hunt remind us that for all our efforts the Holy can come crashing through, or drag us helplessly into its world whether we will it or not. The Hunt reminds us that before the awe inspiring enormity of the Holy, we are very, very, very small and very vulnerable.

With the terror of the Hunt, we are given as well the warmth of the hearth fire, and the beckoning brightness of the festival lights, and the annealing fire of kin and community and, if we are very wise, and very, very courageous, so too we might be given the opportunity to recognize that it is that very vulnerability that makes our humanity so precious in the eyes of the Gods. It is that very vulnerability that makes our triumphs, our failures, our victories, our brave attempts at crafting our world, at living our lives so potentially valorous. With the light born out of the darkness to guide us, we are given the opportunity to re-evaluate our steps and perhaps change the course of our journey. The path and commitments that we have chosen can be illuminated ever more brightly with the darkness behind us; and with the blessings of that darkness and all the terror it holds, the blessings of hearth and home may grow. If we have courage.

Our lives are so much richer, filled with so many more undreamed of luxuries than those of our ancestors. We in the first world need not face this season of cold and dark with the fear of not making it through the winter for lack of warmth, lack of shelter, lack of food. We have enough, more than enough by the reckoning of our ancestors. Famine is far from our door but fear, fear remains. Oh, we may have access to bounty that would make our dead weep, but we still know the cold, gnawing grasp of fear. Is there enough money? Will I still have my job in the New Year? How am I going to pay my rent? My mortgage? Will I be able to afford to buy groceries this week? Will I have to go on foodstamps? How will I survive? Will I ever be able to thrive?

Yule makes us take stock of our abundance and our ability to manage our resources. Thrift was a grace much prized by our ancestors because it ensured their survival and moreover the survival of the next generation. A stable household was a household well-managed, in which resources were not squandered or wasted. This too is part of Yule. It is the civilized portion, that which honors the graces of a well-run home. This is the light that sustains when one must lose oneself temporarily in the darkness.

Ultimately, Yule is about transforming fear: of loss, of hope, of hunger, of lack, of the darkness within our very own selves. It is a time to celebrate what we have, and a call to arms to be mindful that we use it wisely. We celebrate because we have something to celebrate be it only the victory of drawing our next breath. Yule is a time not just to honor our blessings, but to consciously allow them to flow forth from us to those who have helped sustain us in our dark times: friends, family, the stranger on the street perhaps. It is a time to recognize that the darkness comes for us all, but so too does the light.

NEW YEAR

I'm deviating from things Heathen and including House Sankofa's New Year rite. We've a couple of Roman polytheists in our number who specifically requested something for New Year. This is a ritual that many of us will be doing in our own homes as the year turns. This time, our Greco-Roman lineage took the lead with defining the ritual.

Do this so that you begin on the 31st and end on the 1st. Adapt it as you need and wish. Five Deities are invoked: Cardea, the Goddess of the door hinge, Limentius, the God of the threshold, Forculus, God of the doorway, Janus, God of beginnings, doorways, passages, etc. (January is named after Him), and Hermes.

Pre-ritual prep:

Take a ritual bath to prepare yourself and dress in clean clothing.

I. Begin by cleaning all your shrines, both to the Gods and the ancestors.

II. Make an offering to your ancestors, thanking them for all their help and protection in the previous year and asking for their continued blessings.

III. Make an equal offering to the house spirits.

IV. If you have a mask, don it now and take up a noise-maker (drum, rattle, even a can filled with some coins) and open a couple of windows. Go through every room in the house making as much noise as you can, cleansing it via sound of any stagnant or unhelpful or malignant energy. Sweep your house, every room if possible and sweet out the door. Then vacuum. (I'm practical. My mother was Swiss.) Take off the mask and put away the noisemaker.

V. Light four candles and ask the blessing of fire on your home.

VI. Go to the front door. Wipe it, the threshold, and the lintels down with an infusion of juniper or verbena, or some other sweet and cleansing herb (I think Florida Water is a good substitute). Hang colored streamers from your door (colored wool would have been traditional), anoint the hinges with a dab of olive oil. Asperse the door three times with verbena water, Florida Water, rose water or some other sweet smelling infusion. Offer the following prayers. After each prayer, set or pour out an offering glass of wine.

Prayers to Hermes

I sing of Hermes, the favorite of Bakcheios,
the wily one with mischief and wisdom in his heart.
He stands at the cross-roads, a pillar connecting the worlds,
whose foundation is in the underworld
and whose eyes survey all that transpires in heaven.
He is the lord of magic, the inventor of words and religious rites,
the trustworthy one who knows the secrets of the gods
and interprets their will for mankind

In gratitude let my lips pour forth praise
for Hermes, the wily one, the master of many guises
clever in his plotting, who wanders over wide ways
with feet so light they never leave a track
for the huntsman to follow. Ghost-like, shifting,
who flits through our thoughts and knows how
to carry off our deepest, most well-guarded secrets,

King of the land of Sleep who guides the
dreams like sheep through one of the two gates
to find their way to us while our bodies rest,
and with the same staff he uses to check
their step he can conjure illusions and
shape reality to his will, he can cause poisonous
roots to spring up from the earth and brew
strange philters to protect against the witch's charms,
for Hermes is great in magic and the inventor of
powerful words. Those words he knows how to use,
to bend the rules of society and trick the canny
businessman out of his money. Hermes wants for
nothing for through hard work, cleverness, the
weaving of fine tales and simple treachery or theft
he can get whatever it is he wants and even
managed to sneak his way into the bed of the lovely
Aphrodite whose soft, warm flesh delighted him so.
Hail Hermes, is there anything you cannot
accomplish? If so I am ignorant of it.

(prayer by Sannion)

Prayer to Cardea

I call to You,
Sweet Cardea,
Guardian of all passageways.
Without your leave no blessings may flow.
You are guardian and keeper of the earth:
You open that which has been closed,
and close that which has been opened.
Bless us this night and in the year to come
with an abundance of all good things.
To You, gracious Goddess
we pray.

(prayer by Galina)

Prayer to Forculus

I hail You, Forculus,
Gracious Guardian of the door.
I ask Your blessings and protection
on my home and in my life
in the year to come;
and I thank you for
for watching over me
in the year now past.
To You,
doorkeeper of the earth,
I pray.

(prayer by Galina)

Prayer to Limentius

I pray to You, Limentius,
God of the threshold.
I thank You for the grace
of Your protection and care
in the year now past.
I ask that You watch over
and protect me
in the year to come.
To You, keeper of the threshold,
I pray.

(prayer by Galina)

Prayer to Janus

Sing I Ianus,
lord with two faces,
who opens the door,
and causes unexpected things to occur.
To those who have your favor,
no obstacle blocks their path.

You create the way where none appeared before,
and bring helpful spirits through to aid us in our work.
No great task is begun without first invoking you,
gatekeeper of Olympos who holds the keys
to all the temples of the gods.
O Ianus, unlock the door of my mind
to let powerful verse spill forth,
like the Nile in flood season.
O Ianus, unblock the gates of the underworld,
so that Demeter's rich bounty can fill the land.
O Ianus, make smooth the way so that men's prayers may travel up
and reach the ears of the Blessed Immortals.
Ianus I sing!

(prayer by Sannion)

Make the following offerings:

* refried beans (seriously, a traditional dish for Cardea; she likes the ancient Roman equivalent of re-fried beans)
* a bowl of milk and honey
* sweet wine
* fresh water
* bread and butter
* anything else you feel moved to give.

Light a little incense. Hang a wreath on the door and ask for the Gods' protection (if you have hawthorn, this is particularly associated with Cardea and is very protective. Laurel would have also been traditional for these wreaths). Say: "Joy to this house" three times.

VII. Go back inside and give an offering of grain and salt or salt and bread to the fire.

VIII. Eat something sweet, symbolic of welcoming sweetness in the new year. It's also nice if, at this point, you can share a meal, however simple, with those you love

IX. If you have the skill, sit and do divination for the rest of the year. (This is a good time as head of your house to do household divination. You can always follow up with a professional diviner if anything comes up that's troubling or you feel needs to be further addressed.)

X. When you are next out, give food to the poor/homeless/hungry.

MEMORIAL DAY: HONORING OUR WARRIORS

I walk the warrior's path. I have in my time served a Goddess of war (Sekhmet) and I'm owned by a God of war and military leadership (Odin). I've studied martial arts, weapons, shooting, and but for an early back injury, would have gone into the military. I am fortunate that within Heathenry, the values taught along the warrior's path are generally respected. Before I became Heathen, however, when I moved predominantly in eclectic Pagan circles, my respect for those who submit themselves to the discipline of warriorship, and my devotion to Deities specifically associated with war, often made me a rarity.

I had not initially planned to write anything to commemorate Memorial Day. As I began reading the responses to several articles (on various Pagan forums) praising soldiers, or honoring those who have fallen in war – responses full of the sentimentality and arrogance, contempt and ignorance, that only those who never had to defend what they hold dear could summon forth – I felt the need to comment; and I'm going to be fairly blunt.

Warriorship is not what it was. We can kill today by pushing a button. Thousands die for governments that have their heads so far up their asses that we'd need a mining expedition to free them. I believe there is virtue in service, one that lies well outside any ideological or political dogma. Honoring warriors and soldiers has nothing to do with supporting the wars in which they fought. It has everything to do with supporting the courage, discipline, and dedication of those doing the fighting.

Paganism evolved as part of the counter-cultural revolution and as such, many denominations still bear the mark of its influence both for good and for ill. What we've forgotten as we indulge ourselves is that in another age, we wouldn't have a choice but to respect those who put their lives on the line so we don't have to. We have the luxury of disdaining warriorship because we live in a pampered society largely isolated from the horrors that so many people in this world endure every day. Oh, we can read about these things, respond with moral objections to the war du jour, see carnage on CNN, but we're not expecting it to come in our doors. Many of us don't give a passing thought to those who have lived through these horrors – soldiers, medical staff, and civilians alike – and who still wake up in the night having dreamt of those terrors. No one craves peace more than those who have endured war. They're the ones who know the necessity of sacrificing for it.

We owe a debt to our soldiers and veterans. It is a debt that we may never repay. We owe a debt to those Vietnam vets who returned from war to be spat on. We owe a debt to those veterans who live on the street because their countries did nothing to help them transition back into civilian life. We owe a debt to those soldiers consumed by addiction because they've no other way of drowning out the voices of their fallen comrades. We owe a debt to those dead soldiers who fought and died in defense of ideals of freedom and self-determination: who died so that we would have the freedom to turn around and slander them.

Civilization was built on the backs of artisans and farmers. The mortar of that foundation was the blood of those willing to die to see the next generation thrive. That's what warriorship is all about: doing what is necessary to ensure that one's family, tribe, and civilization lives another day. Even when we miss the mark, even when we fail, on an individual level that sacrifice is worthy of respect. When we fail to honor our soldiers, and others who serve in the military, we dishonor every ancestor who ever had to take up arms to defend themselves, their livelihood, their families, children, countries, villages, and tribes. We dishonor all those who bled whether they wanted to or not, in order that we might have a chance for something better. The obligation of respect goes well beyond any ethnic, ideological, political, or social barriers. It's not about whether one agrees with the reason for the fight. But for those willing to stand up, march off and die, a significant number of our ancestors I might add, we wouldn't be here. We reap the benefits of those who came before us; therefore, it is right and proper that we honor them. We live in softer, not more enlightened times. We criticize their choices without any comprehension of the necessities involved.

Having walked the warrior's path for thirty years, I know that there are things that one can learn no other way. This path hones the spirit. It strips away the inessential, it tramples sentimentality and platitudes. It brings an immense freedom to act rightly and well, despite opposition; it teaches courage in the face of mind numbing fear. It teaches endurance and perseverance in the face of agony. It makes one strong from the inside out. Warriors see the worst that humanity has to offer. They experience it firsthand. Some lose their humanity. Some lose themselves. But others become filled with a compassion that is as vast as the stars, as deep as the oceans; and they bring that back to the people they love, and that stone strong compassion begins to inform their every interaction.

Tangentially, I would also add that there are numerous Deities that have battle aspects: Sekhmet, Ishtar, Freya, Skadhi, Scathach, Morrigan, Tyr, Ninshubur, Ares, Odin, Mars, Nuada, to name but a few. The list is much longer. When we dishonor those on this path, we spit in the faces of these Deities as well. The lessons that these Deities have to teach are often the most essential in the modern day.

Essentially, what it comes down to is this: honor your dead. Honor all your dead, not just the ones of whose professions you approved. Give thanks that you don't have to make the same sacrifices, or live the same life that they did. Give thanks that you don't have to fight and bleed and die for a future you never got to see. Give thanks and give them the common courtesy of respect for their part in your being here.

War is a terrible thing, but warriorship is not. Go out and thank a Veteran on Memorial Day. Go lay flowers on the grave of a fallen soldier. Light a candle and thank the Gods you don't have to do what they did. Maybe even light a candle and thank them for their service!

Appendix

One of the things that I often give to students coming to me to learn devotional work is a copy of C.S. Lewis' *Till We Have Faces*. I once heard this book referred to as one of the great pagan novels of the 20th century, for all that Lewis was a devout Christian. The story is that of Eros and Psyche, retold as an allegory for the devotional and spiritual journey. It is a wrenching, powerful tale, defiantly compelling, and I used this book, along with the following questions, with my students for years. I would encourage them to discuss the questions in study groups, and assigned certain of the questions as essays. These were questions that I worked out over twenty years ago with another priest in Iseum of the Star Eyed Warrior for our training program. I provide them here now for your use.

I. Contrast your own conception of the words 'holy' and 'holiness' with:
   A) Orual's citing the context of the following passages and
   B) Other words such as 'spiritual' and 'sacred.'
      Pg 54 "the horror of holiness"
      Pg. 94 "got away from all that holiness"
      Pg. 43 "it became very holy"
      Pg 11 "the holiness of the smell that hung about him."

II. On page 54, despite Orual's vehement differences with the Priest of Ungit's morality, she has to concede in her own mind that the Priest truly believed in Ungit completely.
   A) Does your sense of morality completely come from your spiritual awareness or are there other factors that contribute to it?

B) If your morality, and what you truly believed was your duty commanded by Deity, clashed, how would you seek balance again? And which would win out?

C) If Ungit truly told the priest that Psyche (Istra) was the chosen sacrifice, this would also benefit the Priest by ridding Glome of a believed Goddess incarnate on earth that could possibly usurp his power. Being Orual, how would you feel about both realities existing simultaneously?

III. On page 71–76, Istra's opening of her spiritual consciousness in her most desperate hour offers her a comfort to which Orual cannot possibly relate.

A) Why is crisis often associated with spiritual awakening?

B) Orual expresses jealousy over Istra's increasing spiritual awakening seemingly eclipsing the intensity and significance of the relationship between Istra and herself. How do you balance one's complete devotion to the Deities with all your relationships with others on the mortal plane?

IV. How does the motivation behind the King's god-fearing ways differ from Bardia's and how do these different motivations affect the progress of their spiritual growth? With which do you more closely identify?

V. On page 94, in the second paragraph, a ritual is described in which a priest, every spring, is shut up inside the House of Ungit only to fight his way out through the temple's western door again much like a newborn fighting his way out of the womb of the mother.

A) How is the awakening along the spiritual road like a birthing from the womb?

B) When a baby first comes into the world, it cries. Tears are also often associated with intense spiritual connections or visions of the Divine. What is the significance of this similarity?

C) The attempted sacrifice of Psyche (Istra) through death to please the Deities and bring to the kingdom of Glome good fortune became to her a kind of spiritual awakening where she perceived a God face to face. How is the awakening along the spiritual road like a birthing from a tomb?

D) As it relates to your own perception of the spiritual journey, what do these elements of the ritual sacrifice of Psyche (Istra) represent or mean to you?:

    1. The chosen site of the ritual being a mountain

    2. The mountain's name/color being 'grey'

    3. The tree to which Psyche (Istra) was tied

    4. The tying of Psyche (Istra) to the tree by the waist with hands and feet free.

    5. The iron chains used to tie Psyche (Istra) to the tree

    6. The period of Psyche's (Istra's) solitude after the ritual was performed.

VI. The opening two lines of the book immediately cast the Gods in an adversarial position against Orual (at least in her mind). Compare and contrast Orual's bitter and fearful approach to the Gods with that of Istra's passionate enchantment.

A) What was the catalyst between them leading to the different approaches?

B) How do you feel about the extreme fatalism which overlays each character's interactions with the Divine realm?

C) How do you feel about the concept of the Gods as adversaries?

D) Can one have a deep, rewarding and intimate relationship with the Gods while at the same time seeing Them as potential or actual adversaries?

VII. The twin concepts of fear and jealousy recur consistently upon mention of the Gods especially Ungit. What lies behind this recurring fear of Divine jealousy? Would you say that the people in the book, project their own jealousies and fears onto the Divine? How does this possibly impact both Orual's and Istra's approach to the Divine?

VIII. On page 4, the Goddess Ungit is referred to as being alone. In their respective isolation/aloneness, it appears that Orual unconsciously mirrors the harshest visage of Ungit.

A) Why do you think she does so?

B) What purpose does this serve both for the Goddess, for Orual and those who interact with them?

C) Would you agree with her interpretation of Ungit's nature or do you think it was solely her own perception and bitterness speaking?

IX. On page 49, Lewis writes "Some say loving and devouring are all the same thing."

A) What do you think is meant by that statement?

B) Explore that within the confines of the relationship between Orual and Istra. Do you agree or disagree with it?

C) How do you think it impacted Orual's response to Istra's spiritual awakening?

D) How would you apply that to your own relationship with the Divine?

X. The King's reaction when his second wife, though dead from the effort, bore him only a daughter, the King's treatment of all his daughters, how Ungit and Aphrodite (especially in the tale on page 8) are perceived and the personality of Batta all contribute to a definite conditioning of the feminine persona in the Kingdom of Glome.

A) Within the Kingdon of Glome, how are women perceived and how might these perceptions influence:

1. Male citizens' concept of the Feminine Divine?

2. Female citizens' concept of the Feminine Divine?

B) What in your own life do you believe influences your concept of the Divine?

C) How do you balance the concept of a specific Deity within the context of an established religion against how that Deity may personally come to you?

XI. A specific dynamic is established in the relationship between Orual and her father when she refers to him more often as King than father. How may your praise names for your Deities influence your perception of Them in your spiritual awakening?

Till We Have Faces Chapters 11-21

1. How do you feel about the concept of the Gods as lovers? Why do you think this is integral to the mystical experience? How does it impact your understanding of the Divine? Of the concept of love and faith?

2. Which do you identify more strongly with: Orual or Istra? Why?

3. What do you consider more important: scholarly knowledge about a God/dess or direct experience with that God/dess? What do you do when the two differ significantly?

4. When Orual could not perceive with her five senses the beautiful palace on the mountain that Psyche called her new home, Orual toyed with the idea Psyche might be mad. By what criteria do you determine a spiritual belief to be an insane one?

5. Between Orual's first and second visit with Psyche on the mountain, her mind vacillated between Psyche just being insane, Psyche being ensnared by some horrible demon or otherworldly monster, Psyche being in the clutches of some vagrant living on the mountain taking advantage of her insane sate, or Psyche truly having a Divine Lover and holy palace. Confusion, fear, and anger may be reasonable reactions to all of this, yet even before all these thoughts were fully realized, Orual felt hatred for all only Psyche could perceive. Why hatred?

6. Though between the two of them Psyche was the one who could see, hear, smell, touch, and taste all, Orual would accuse her of blind faith where her Divine lover was concerned.

a) If blind means unable to see, what are people of blind faith not seeing?

b) Considering what you believe 'faith' to be, is there such a thing as unblind faith?

7. At twilight, when Orual went to fetch a drink from the ice cold river on the mountain, she thought for an instant she could perceive Psyche's palace. Why do you think this sighting probably occurred at this particular time?

8. In a desperate attempt to force Psyche to betray her Divine Lover, Orual cut herself deeply in the arm with a dagger, then threatened to take both Psyche's and her own life if Psyche did not comply. If someone you loved or cared about took such desperate measures to force you to betray your Gods (Deities), how would you react?

9. If you were Orual on the mountain with Psyche talking on and on about her invisible palace and Divine lover which you could not perceive, how would you have reacted?

10. When Psyche betrays her Divine Lover by stealing a peek at Him by the flame of a lantern, the God appears to Orual solemnly proclaiming both she and Psyche would be made to wander in the wilderness in exile like bloodsisters.

a) How did Orual also become Psyche?

b) Which do you believe to be worse: knowing your betrayal of your God may mean never having a mystical communion with Him again; or the existence of a God (and take this to mean Deity in all forms/all Gods) with which you may never have a mystical communion?

11) Which do you believe to be a more desirable love:

a) A love which compels one to provide you with al necessary to make your life plaesant, comfortable, and enjoyable or

b). A love which compels one to injure themselves and you in order to save you from yourself, though with much internal heartache?

12. How is Deity's love harsh and how is it kind?

13. Have you ever felt Divine love completing with mortal love and how did you resolve the situation? How do you feel that situation should be resolved?

14.

a) Why do you think Psyche's Divine Lover hid His face from her?

b) What do you think prompted Orual's decision to only go out in public veiled?

c) Are there any aspects of the Divine that seem hidden to you and why do you think they are so?

d) Are there any aspects of yourself you wish you could hide from Deity?

15. Both the Fox and Bardia seemed content to adhere to their own beliefs about the Deities without either challenging Them face to face or cultivating a one-on-one relationship with Them.

a) Why do you think each one was wary of becoming too close to the Deities?

b) Can one *be* too close to one's Gods?

c) Why is developing a mystical communion with the Deities sometimes feared?

d) Describing from the most influential on down, what are your relevant sources of information when it comes to the Gods? Why and why that particular order?

16. Orual, at one point in the story, called upon the Gods directly with no sacrifice nor in the confines of a sacred temple to show her a sign of Their existence, pledging with all her heart to abide Their wishes. She claimed she received no such sign.

a) When people ask for a sign from the Gods, what sort of phenomenon are they usually expecting, in your opinion?

b) What was the most extraordinary moment when you truly felt Deity upon you?

c) What was the most *un*-extraordinary moment when you truly felt Deity upon you?

d) When Orual delivered the fatal cut to Argan's leg in the battle dictating the fate of Trunia, what did she simultaneously cut out in:

1. Herself as defined by the outside world?
2. Herself as defined by her own soul?

Recommended Resources

Talking to the Spirits by Kenaz Filan and Raven Kaldera
Dealing with Deities by Kenaz Filan and Raven Kaldera
Enduring Grace by C. Flinders
Spiritual Emergency by Grof and Grof
Candles in the Cave: Northern Tradition Paganism for Prisoners by
    Raven Kaldera
Neolithic Shamanism by Raven Kaldera and Galina Krasskova
Northern Tradition for the Solitary Practitioner by Raven Kaldera and
    Galina Krasskova
Honoring the Ancestors: A Basic Guide by Galina Krasskova
Till We Have Faces by C.S. Lewis
The Screwtape Letters by C.S. Lewis
Walking the Heartroad by Silence Maestas
Miasma by Robert Parker
Spiritual Protection by Sophie Reicher
Dwelling on the Threshold by Sarah Kate Istra Winter

About Galina Krasskova

Galina Krasskova is a Heathen (Norse polytheist) and has been a priest of Odin and Loki since the early nineties. Originally ordained in the Fellowship of Isis in 1995, Ms. Krasskova also attended the oldest interfaith seminary in the U.S. – the New Seminary – where she was ordained in 2000 and where she worked as Dean of Second Year Students for the Academic year of 2011-2012. She is the head of House Sankofa, a member of the Thiasos of the Starry Bull, a member of Asatru in Frankfurt (Frankfurt am Main, Germany), the First Kingdom Church of Asphodel (MA), the American Academy of Religion, and the Religious Coalition for Reproductive Choice. Beyond this, she took vows as a Heathen gythia in 1996 and again in 2004.

Ms. Krasskova holds diplomas from The New Seminary (2000), a B.A. in Cultural Studies with a concentration in Religious Studies from Empire State College (2007), and an M.A. in Religious Studies from New York University (2009). She's presented at prestigious academic conferences including those held at Harvard, Santa Barbara University, and Ohio State University. Her Master's thesis, titled "Race, Gender, and the Problem of 'Ergi' in Modern Heathenry" explored concepts of gender roles within contemporary Heathen ritual structure and their impact on contemporary ideological fault lines. She is currently pursuing her Ph.D. in Classics.

An experienced diviner, ordeal master, and conjure woman, her primary interests are in restoring Heathenry as an indigenous religion, developing a thriving ancestor cultus, devotional work, and the reconstruction of Northern Tradition shamanism. Her book *The Whisperings of Woden* was the landmark first devotional text to be written in modern Heathenry. In addition to her own books, she's also contributed extensively to Raven Kaldera's shamanism series.

Ms. Krasskova co-hosts (with Dionysian and author Sannion), a bi-monthly radio podcast: Wyrd Ways Radio. She has a variety of published books available running the gamut from introductory texts on the Northern Tradition, to books on runes, prayer, and devotional practices, with more books on the way. She is also the managing editor of *Walking the Worlds*, a new journal focusing on contemporary polytheism and spiritwork (see walkingtheworlds. wordpress.com). While very busy with teaching and school, she does also occasionally lecture around the country on topics of interest to contemporary Heathenry and polytheisms. For more information, please contact her directly at krasskova@gmail.com.

Other Titles by Sanngetall Press

He is Frenzy: Collected Writings on Odin
Transgressing Faith: Race, Gender, and the Problem of 'Ergi' in Modern American Heathenry
Consuming Flame: A Devotional Anthology for Loki and His Family
Dancing in the House of the Moon: A Devotional for the Moon God Mani
Honoring the Ancestors: A Basic Guide

Also by Galina Krasskova

Numinous Places (blurb.com)
Neolithic Shamanism (Inner Traditions, with Raven Kaldera)
Essays in Modern Heathenry (Asphodel Press)
Runes: Theory and Practice (New Page Books)
Exploring the Northern Tradition (New Page Books)
Northern Tradition for the Solitary Practitioner (New Page Books, with Raven Kaldera)
Feeding the Flame: A Devotional to Loki and His Family (Asphodel Press)
The Whisperings of Woden (Asphodel Press)
Root, Stone, and Bone: Honoring Andvari and the Vaettir of Money (Asphodel Press, with Fuensanta Arismendi)

Sigyn: Our Lady of the Staying Power (Asphodel Press)
Sekhmet: When the Lion Roars (Asphodel Press)
Into the Great Below: A Devotional for Inanna and Ereshkigal
    (Asphodel Press)
A Child's Eye View of Heathenry (Spero Press)
Honoring Sigyn: the Norse Goddess of Constancy (Spero Press)
Sigdrifa's Prayer: An Exploration and Exegesis (Asphodel Press)
Skalded Apples: A Devotional Anthology for Idunna and Bragi
    (Asphodel Press)
Walking Toward Yggdrasil (Asphodel Press)
Full Fathom Five (Asphodel Press)
Day Star and Whirling Wheel (Asphodel Press)

Made in the USA
Coppell, TX
23 December 2020

47030508R00118